Jeron Charles Criswell King

Edwin Lee Canfield, Editor

Charles Phillip Wireman, Assistant Editor

Bear Manor Media

Cover Design & Book Layout by GERVO™

Published in the USA by
Bear Manor Media
1317 Edgewater Dr #110
Orlando FL 32804
www.BearManorMedia.com

Softcover Edition
ISBN-10:
ISBN-13: 979-8-88771-258-1

Published in the USA by Bear Manor Media 

DEDICATION

Who knows but what future generations from some other planet will dig down through seven layers of rubble and find us some 2,000 years hence, crowd around a museum glass containing a broken fragment of a Coca Cola bottle, a bent hairpin and a parched copy of our Bible which managed to escape the terrifying destruction of our civilization! They will wonder what on earth was meant by the words "Henry Ford or "Hollywood" and what in heaven's name was a Criswell?

Jeron Charles Criswell King

August 18, 1907 - October 4, 1982

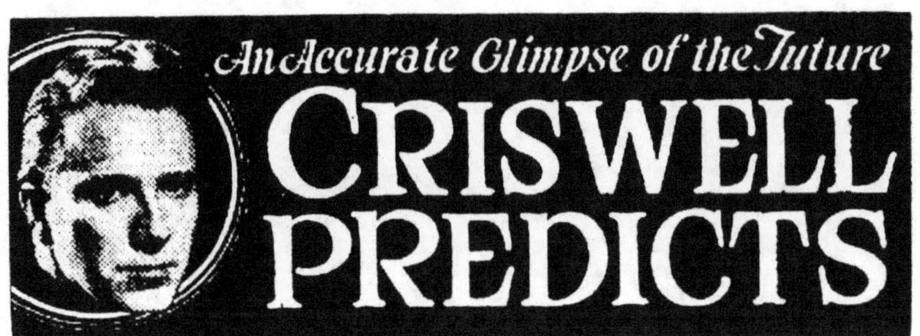

CONTENTS

Acknowledgments..1

Preface...2

We're 10 Seconds from Eternity!...3

PREDICTIONS

Coffee, Commies, Carnage, Chaos, Crisis, Civil Rights, and Climate Change.............4

Politics and Scandal...20

People, Places, Things, and Headlines of the Future......................38

Sexxx, Nudism, UFOs, and Outer Space.....................................60

Ghosts of Hollywood..69

For Women Only!..84

Rock & Roll, Robbery, Riot, Rape, Revelry, and Drugs.....................89

ESSAYS

Criswell's Hall of Shame for Crimes Against Womanhood...................100

Criswell Predicts Climate Change!......................................114

Flying Saucers Over Hollywood..120

Criswell Predicts 1999!..127

Criswell Returns from the Grave..140

Epilogue...149

Afterword..150

About the Editors..151

ACKNOWLEDGMENTS

Predictions from *Quote-The Weekly Digest* by Public Speakers Press, Inc. Anderson, SC 1970-76

Illustrations by Lewis N. Schilling, Jr. from

Criswell Predicts from Now to the Year 2000! and

Your Next Ten Years—Criswell Predicts!

"This 20th Century Nostradamus has a life that truly belongs to the public, for he has dedicated himself to the problems of mankind and how they can be solved in the future." Charles Wireman

PREFACE

Criswell's relative fame in the early stages of the mass-media era was an innocent, harmless symptom of the beginning and continuation of the blurring of the razor-thin line between News with factual information and Entertainment fiction disguised as News in the late-twentieth century. That line has now been all but obliterated in the twenty-first century. His willingness to merely "make things up" and pass them off as the truth and also proclaim himself a success, even after continuous relative failures, shows some of the original, seemingly innocuous roots of the current societal climate of harmful and unrestrained fake news, alternative facts, and conspiracy theories. The spread of unintentional and intentional misinformation and disinformation aided by the exponential growth of information and media access has led to the current sad state of affairs of an unquenchable thirst for infotainment. Not facts. The old and wise adage of, "Don't be so quick to believe what you hear because lies spread faster than the truth." and the often incorrectly attributed to Mark Twain quote, "A lie can travel around the world and back again while the truth is lacing up its boots." couldn't be truer now and shows no sign of slowing in the future.

Charles Phillip Wireman, Assistant Editor

We're 10 Seconds from Eternity!

Yes, my friend, we are all ten seconds from Eternity! For in ten seconds the vitality can leave the body and we are well beyond medical science! Watchmen, what of the night? Friend, what of the future? Traveler, what of the road ahead? 1972 will be a stormy year! Point of no return! We are all on the treadmill to oblivion and we shall arrive in time! As we move across the huge checkerboard of night and days we have no time for meditation, only time to live each second! We live in a world that is getting smaller and smaller and receive a message from the moon in split second timing! We are so closely knit by the printed word, the spoken word of radio and television and our own telephone system undreamed of half a century ago! Time is speeding up and we are reaching the end of our time! We have so much to look forward to…the shocking styles of next year…the steam driven automobile and the electric motor will make gasoline a thing of the past…the new mobile living cult with our homes folding out of an automobile…personalized wings with which to fly in safety…new items will make our jaded living more exciting than ever before…a television screen in third dimension which will cover your entire wall…a tiny radio we may place in our ear…a mechanical regulator which will keep our body in tip top shape—but most of all a built in mental computer which will keep you on your good behavior, keep you from saying nasty things, regulate your diet and food intake and keep you happy!

Coffee, Commies, Carnage, Chaos, Crisis, Civil Rights, and Climate Change!

U.S. TO TURN AWAY FROM COFFEE? Madison Avenue and Coffee: Criswell predicts that slowly but surely America will turn away from coffee, and that a price war on coffee will be the only answer, where coffee again is made inexpensive. Free coffee will be given in restaurants and the popularity of coffee will be touted by Madison Avenue which will spend millions of dollars in ad space to get America back in the coffee drinking habit.

Carnage, chaos and crisis for the Kremlin late next year where the streets of Moscow will run blood like water after a spring rain! The Malcontents of Communism who are not winning rapidly enough all over the world will stage a minor revolution inside the Kremlin! Even Russia cannot stand permissive anarchy, and the fomenters will be struck down! Remember this prediction! I predict that some of our crazy people of our sane society will try to establish a new nation in Cuba of free souls and sexually disarranged virtues, which will even enrage the now Communist way of thinking! Castro will personally ask that this movement be stopped!…American manufacturers will be most excited by the introduction of a new screw cap for soft drinks and food items, low cost and easy to use, making disposable containers easy to discard.

Every tick of the clock brings us nearer and nearer to our Grand Destination! It could be tomorrow—next week—or next year! Our geologists working overtime shake their heads and ponder, each giving a dire prediction of the Grand Destination!...Residue in the Wabash! Yes, for the first time in history there is a mysterious residue in the Wabash River near Mount Carmel, Illinois! This murky goo from the core of the earth threatens to clog up the flowing river and destroy the new catfish hatchings!

When Nostradamus predicted about our 20th century, he listed one hundred events to happen between 1975 and 1999. Here is the predicted Event No. 46 "The orbit of the earth will be affected by the continual chanting of complaint until a listing is noticed, and the off-gravity effect will cause people to fall across the street sideways and result in much injury!" This prediction coincides with what the Geologists claim will happen, the sudden lessening of gravity and the tumbling of objects on the earth, even people!

In his safe secure world of 1544, Nostradamus issued his famous "Centuries" in which he listed 100 events to happen in the world from 1975 to 1999! We list these in our latest book *Forbidden Predictions of Nostradamus*, which heads the best seller lists in many cities. Here is the predicted Event 77: "This deadly disease will be a cancerous skin growth which within ten days will completely shred the skin from the body leaving only a sagging, bloody flesh!

In my latest book *The Forbidden Predictions of Nostradamus*, I have listed the 100 events to happen between 1975 and 1999, including: Churches and other quiet places will be crowded with the saddened madding crowds seeking solace and quietness of personal sanctuary...Huge blocks of ice will block the harbors of every port in the world making navigation almost impossible...The law of gravity will begin to lose effect and the air will be filled with chunks of ice making air travel dangerous and foolhardy.

Coffee will be 10 percent cheaper in 1971 due to bumper crops and new processing methods...Try as they may, chemists can never find a true substitute for milk...Shaggy hair and beards will be banned from schools and colleges because too many diseases are breeding in this personal filth...Madam Death will ride the highways and airways this year with a vengeance.

Many of you who saw me with Tom Snyder on New Year's Eve following the Johnny Carson Show, wrote me about my prediction "that men would take the pill" and that they will, as they can trust themselves and would not let the pill slip their minds!...Undersea volcanoes will be in your weather news as they happen frequently off the coast of California, Louisiana and the Virginias! Many of the innocent looking oil blobs are belched from the bowels of the Earth and not from the ships!

A wave of despair will strike Poland, and not one promise made by Russia In the recent treaty will be kept...USA faces invasion of roaches, immune to most any preparation. Remember, ten minutes after Hiroshima was atom bombed, the area was crawling with millions of roaches...Many thousands of American tourists will be stranded in South America due to revaluation of the currency by sudden change of governments to communism.

I predict that the old days of a gasoline price war will soon return in many areas...the American tourist will face brutal insults when in foreign nations due to the Anti-American feeling now being generated out of Europe and Asia. Uncle Sam is Uncle Sap...Queen Elizabeth II will face a royal battle over the reduction of expense funds. "Pomp and Circumstance" does not come cheap. Her health is not the best and she will ponder abdication in favor of her son, who would be King Charles III.

I predict that under-sea volcanoes will terrify Canada and also Alaska...food prices will decline a full ten percent by mid-year...Internal Revenue Service will declare war on the known tax evaders...Three heads of government, three members of our Supreme Court, three well-loved and famous mayors and five famous show business personalities will die before deep winter...a new series of events will open the closed minds of Americans as never before.

I predict that Wall Street will boast of a Dow Jones average of 1500 by July, 1976…Export and import will boom as never before…building and land sales will boom population will flow to suburban areas in a huge avalanche…bankrupt cities will be a fact…Will Russia and China, the two communist sisters, band together with England?…We are on the edge of betrayal by our so-called friends…Shocking things are about to happen…we cannot invent the future, for it is out there waiting to happen!

I predict that Russia and China will hold a joint purge of all the dissidents in their realms, by firing squad…waves of the future will bring welfare by computer, with dishonest recipients being sent to jail…that facial rejuvenation for men and women will be the next rage…that heavy protection will be given all political candidates due to the permissiveness of the present campaign…a magical liquid fertilizer will restore tired land to life…that George Bernard Shaw's life will be filmed in London.

I predict a famine in India, a tidal wave in Japan an earthquake in Alaska, a cascade of water spouts off the New Jersey coast, a volcano eruption in Greece, a festival in Venice, a Holy Year in Rome, a boom in Florida, a revolution in Cuba, a royal battle between the British and the Irish, a bloodletting in Central Africa and outright murder on the football field due to the use of drugs in sports to a fatal degree. Sports idol after sports idol will die due to drug addiction.

I predict that we are entering a period of crisis, carnage and confusion…the next musical star to light the theatrical heavens will be Panfilo, whose rare talent will take him far…Panfilo will remind you of Sinatra…a practical and simple male sterilization program will win wide acceptance…this operation will be performed on prisoners, discharged convicts, mental cases and wayward juveniles…America will soon be free from the coffee combine with the raising of "wild coffee" in Arizona and New Mexico…we are on the verge of free burial service through a new Federal Nixon law.

The winds of chance will dry up and destroy the water life in the Mediterranean. The odor will sicken the inhabitants and in time this will be worldwide. This blight will reach into the forests and will result in a famine for the animal kingdom! The fifteen lakes in the middle of America will become so oil infested they will blaze with untold suffering!…The safety box of gold in Middle America will be stormed by foreigners but the gold and silver will not be removed. That Fort will stand as a symbol of power…When we consider the forecast of this remarkable prophet where he mentions the control of weather by chemicals, the present algae in the Mediterranean and our drought in the Midwest and Fort Knox, he was indeed remarkable! No other prophet has been so accurate!

I predict that before 1973 becomes history, we will have a day of national emergency, resembling but not quite like Pearl Harbor…Welfare will cease except for the elderly and the maimed…narcotics will vanish instantly a new branch of science has inverted growth whereby a plant can be taken and reverted to a seed...a beautiful haven of nature with a lake, old western town, campgrounds and stables located in California will soon delight you on your TV screen.

I predict an evil air of pollution will move up from the Gulf of Mexico, smothering and obliterating life in many Mexican cities! Terror will ride the air waves in a most frightening manner. Our nation will be spared for the time being in this deluge!...China and Russia will be the culprits in the destruction of many of the sacred sites in the Holy Land which will leave an aching heart the world over...The Red Sea will be strangely affected by undersea volcanoes and coast lines will change overnight!

I predict a price war on gasoline from Maine to California before 1975 becomes history. The Arab Oil combine will be dissolved through petty politics and will vanish into thin air...Expect bitter backstage battles to take place in the UN...organized looting of homes, offices and stores will terrorize the nation and will speed the police state Texas will reinstate the death penalty which will reduce car theft as death will become the penalty for car theft.

When Madame History records 1974 she will call it a year of crisis, chaos and carnage...martial law will be declared in Chicago to stem the tide of crime...battery powered bikes will crowd our highways and byways...educational standards will hit a new low in three years and many high school graduates will be unable to read and write...the new lifting of the rules on the search-and-seizure laws will bring about thousands of narcotic arrests.

A plague in 1973 of flying insects (invisible), a potent deadly wave of bacteria that affect the heart and lungs...The new Panama Canal will not evolve as planned, there will be a different location for it...Many famous companies will move out of NYC...The sex exploitation books are dying a miserable and timely death.

Wife of a Southern governor will be put in a mental institution because of her delight in setting fire to public buildings...Violent storms forecast soon for West Coast of Mexico and USA...Our beloved Nation will be called "Vulgaria," not America, in foreign press because of our vulgar entertainment.

Narcotic addition has turned one of our greatest stars into a vegetable, and his death will come very soon...I predict that the Russian navy will be very evident in Cuba this summer and can be seen off our Fla. Coast any time; the short temper of the Kremlin will move into Cuba for a quick and fatal kill...There will be troops in the streets to restore authority for many areas before summer ends.

I predict the rising rate suicide among atheistic and materialistic college and university students will throw fear into the hearts of our nation...Many of these students will break themselves in their efforts to break the establishment...the restlessness of Japan, China, Russia, Germany, Italy, France, Spain and the Middle East all point to another war...Zsa Zsa Gabor will soon embark on a new marriage and a new career.

The day of the "unbathed" at colleges is coming to a close...A famed soap will vanish from stores because of a boycott by irate housewives over an anti-religious attack by a national commentator...A 10 o'clock curfew in New York to combat street murders...Blood will flow in the gutters of Red Square (Moscow) like water after summer rain.

I predict that four out of every five college students who took a government loan to continue their education will go into a bankrupt condition so they will escape this honorable debt. I predict this will put an end to education financed by the Federal Government! The colleges and universities were only successful in turning out dyed-in-the-wool deadbeats!...I predict that faith healers will be accepted due to the fact that many medicine men in Asia, Africa and South America have been paid through our American welfare!

I predict the Communist takeover of Viet Nam and Cambodia will be 100 percent—with the Shrines being stripped of all the gold and jewels, the movies and bars closed, only one newspaper for sale, all private business turned over to the Commissar, public decapitations for entertainment, all money and jewelry seized, no radio, telephones and no electricity!...the motion picture-television combined strike which will tie up the entertainment world around October 1st!

USA will have close escape from destiny in Vietnam...Red Russia and China will combine and march into India, dividing that poor unfortunate country as Nazi Germany did Poland in 1939...New train plan will be big success and quick, clean travel, good food and service will delight every heart in America...Doris Day will immortalize Carrie Nation in rousing TV musical this fall.

I regretfully predict a coming day of national emergency, when we will suffer another Pearl Harbor. The Gods of War are stirring in the East. Every man, woman and child in America will be called to the colors. Colleges and univs will be closed for the duration. This will be no bonfire war...Booze wagons will soon deliver cold beer and mixed cocktails to homes, just as the ice wagon came around in the old days.

I predict that Cuba will rise again from her Red Masters strangle-hold during the next five years...Queen Elizabeth will find British taxpayers grumbling about her demanded increase for the cost of royal pomp...the new federal rental laws will protect the landlord as he pays more taxes than renters...Miami and Miami Beach will slowly turn into a year-round resort.

I predict that many missing husbands who leave their families for welfare benefits or who flee from the law will be located through social security information becoming public…Russia will withdraw the "welcome mat" for outsiders as too many Russians are becoming interested in our American way of life…Florida will introduce a law which will forbid any overpricing of food, rent or any item to any tourist, resulting in a new tourist boom in that state.

I predict that all Aliens within the borders of this country will be asked to register within the next 90 days! Hush-Hush: A plot will be uncovered which will endanger the safety of America and our house must be set in order!…We will hear the rumble of war drums by September 18th which we will echo worldwide! The mills of the Gods will grind us out another hellish bonfire!…Pay strict attention to diet and rest, for you are under a strain!

UNCENSORED: I predict that at the turn of a card the entire picture of America will change! We will go into a preparation for war, exactly as we did in 1939! Citizens who are now aimlessly floating around living on welfare, will be organized and placed into war materials! It is far too late to turn back as we are propelled into full amazement by Russia, by China, by the Arab Nations and by all others! America will wake up the world by announcing that "Uncle Sam" is no longer "Uncle Sap."

I predict that many city dwellers who are living on welfare will be drafted to harvest crops in a coming work crisis! Our farmers need aid and need it badly…the next triumph of Materia Medica will be the import of humans from Russia with glass encased brains so the action and reaction can be carefully observed by our medical schools. The entire skull is removed and replaced with glass and the unfortunate patient looks like something from a Science-Fiction movie.

The Akashic Record, an endless ribbon of time reveals as it rolls like a reel of film: The Vatican will close…a gentle communism but much more vicious will spread over the world…America will save England from communism and later rule the Mother Country…the Earth will crack due to the pressure of stress beneath the oceans and lost continents will appear!

I predict that many County Fairs and State Fairs will face a mob of unruly activists seeking to destroy the Establishment…I predict that the market will be flooded with many "escape" books which will give you the conditions all over the world for living freely and inexpensively…I predict that Chicago Theater will soon present *Little Women* with an all-male cast…I predict that a new skin cleanser made of cactus oils will be the next cosmetic rage.

I predict a shocking turn of events for the betterment of the nation…A national tragedy will strike the very heart of America which will unite us strongly, clearly and happily…We will no longer apologize but be proud once again…Rather than selling America short we will zoom into a new national pride…I predict that many of the so-called low-cost flights to Europe will prove to be one woe after another.

"Storms sweep north Atlantic coastal areas"…"Suicide of Hollywood star shocks world of entertainment"…"Cholera epidemic spreads from Asia terrifying the world of medicine"…"Artificial impregnation voted illegal in Kentucky"…"Brutal murders in Cuba over new Anti-Castro Plot"…"Gasoline price war shocks nation as prices tumble"…"Earthquake in Nevada".

I predict there will be some behind-the-scenes action where Russia is concerned. The Kremlin will secretly build up Havana as the new Kremlin and make Cuba a stronghold for Communism…the mystery of Castro deepens as rumors fly that he has been replaced by a double…that the trend in Black Betterment will be "separate but equal" in housing, schools and welfare projects because the present urge to integrate has failed to sustain the Black desires.

I predict that the winding river of events will soon bring us face to face with (1) A famed actor and his identical twin brother will face the wrath of outrageous fortune next year with their illegal fast footwork. A shabby collection of phony alibis has saved them so far. (2) The Black Betterment will demand free tickets all attractions. No refusal of any credit to any minority for any reasons will be tolerated. This will be very soon established and carried out to the letter of the new law.

I predict you will witness a murder on the football field in November, in full view of your close-up television camera...you will soon read about the professor who gave his own mother's body to a medical school and then gleefully dissected it before his students...Prayer will soon be back in the Public Schools in addition to the Pledge of Allegiance...There will be further purloined Pentagon papers...Vigilante Laws will soon be in effect in England and Ireland, resulting in Ireland's complete freedom from the Crown and monetary independence.

I predict that the Black Betterment League will demand that the children of Senators and Congressmen attend public schools along with their children in Washington, DC...the new trend in England will be to enlist in the army any employee of the local, state or national government...newsletters will soon explore the new ruling demanded by members of Congress against seniority. It is certain that 11 elected officials do not have seniority, the employees in private industry would no longer enjoy it either.

I predict that vandalism and desecration will grow to an all-time high, with copper graveside vases, marble figures and statuary being sold at high prices, and many states will make it a felony to desecrate any memorial park, church or funeral home…By this time next year a broadcast of nerve gas, resulting in collapse of the human body for 24 hours, will be possible. This broadcast can be directed to a certain point, paralyzing an entire city at once.

In 1971 fire will break out below the Earth's surface. Lakes will become almost solid oil, there will be flaming lakes of fire as all Hell breaks loose…new series of campus bombing will bring many arrests and convictions…Relations between Russia, China and USA will worsen…Jan 18, 1985, many thousands of proud Britishers joined a plague of suicides…Dec 11, 1972, the Mason-Dixon line became a reality again…Dec 13, 1972, a woman dictator seized all power in France.

I predict that more Black parents are against busing than White parents, as it takes their children away from their control…Integrated education is not looked upon with favor as Black History and other culture is omitted 100 percent…Expect violence out of Latin America…Famed actor suicide on Broadway…Florida faces new land boom…New police measures due for Washington, DC…Tragedy strikes noted political family. Everyone who has ever lived in Hollywood invited back to a gigantic Home Coming in September.

I predict a world-wide orgy of weather…a world-wide orgy of spending…a worldwide orgy of total dependence on computers…the Baron of Baseball will not live out another season…the despair of drugs will reach a new crisis in 1973…the present Dow Jones 1000 averages will hold during most of 1973, making Wall Street history…it will soon be learned that many tourists have leprosy contamination from central Africa.

Politics and Scandal

FABULOUS GOSSIP—I predict we will enter an era of fabulous gossip about the famous and the near-famous of the world. A new type of confidential magazine based on court records will be the most read magazine of the year. I predict that three predictions from my book, *Your Next Ten Years*, will be denounced from the pulpits of America, and rightly so. This predicts where many of our spiritual leaders are found wanting. I predict that the new radio "Speak-Your-Mind" shows will not permit the commentator to offer his views, but only be a sounding board for the listener. I predict that Paris will fade in favor of the tourist due to the new "tourist fee for entry," and the gouging prices of the past summer. I predict that the next new super star will be Roger Paris and his one-man show.

The Church and State will be separated into two distinct parts...The greatest change will be on the subject of Christmas...no longer will lighted trees be placed on public buildings...The only place you will find the Christmas spirit will be in your church...
I predict there will be three new active political parties in our nation: Labor, patterned after the British Labor party; the under 21 voters; and the Black Empire, composed of all the blacks, with a full slate of candidates and working with their own money to win.

I predict that a trusted American TV star—athlete will shame his country and profession by selling top secrets to foreign powers...that an international charity will be found spurious, with the scandal reaching all over the world...every dollar they have collected so far has been used for salaries for employees...price control will be very much in the news, with shocking news coming out of Mexico on this subject.

I predict that Patricia Nixon will tell her story in a fantastic autobiography which will be an all-time best seller! Only the wife of President Nixon would know of the despair the victories the happiness and the defeats in the life of this 20th century political miracle...
I predict that there is further heartbreak ahead for Rose Kennedy for one woe will tread on another's heel! This brave and noble woman has had more than her share of agony and personal sorrow.

I regret to predict that the mad dogs of revenge will roam the world again when three leaders of the world will meet death through their fateful assassination...air tragedies will soon multiply through hi-jacking...one tragedy will follow another until a crisis is reached in the United Nations there will be increasing mental illness due to the stress of modern-day living...a sensational murder out of Washington, DC will crowd all news off the front pages for months.

I predict a series of violent anti-United Nations moves in early 1973 by many countries affected by the UN's lack of action in important matters such as the Munich murders, etc. ...heavy Atlantic storms will sweep the Eastern coast in November...London stage plays will need extra police protection against shocking robberies during intermissions…that Rome airports will have radar protection against high-jackers…Mexico City will have its biggest tourist season on record.

Just as the League of Nations carried its own executioner, I predict that the United Nations will come to a sudden and dramatic end. When the Communist Bloc can no longer profit they will withdraw in a body and America will lower the curtain overnight…I predict that the fluctuating stock market will be calmed by the good news out of Washington in March…More states will consider the "painless" revenue from gambling.

I predict that a quiet, desperate campaign will soon take place in the world of television and radio! Madison Avenue and the sponsors will demand more conservative programming as the ultra-liberal programming does not sell merchandise and the advertising money is wasted! I predict that several of the super-star commentators and newscasters will refuse certain commercials on their programs which will hasten the decision on the part of the networks!

I predict that 1972 and 1973 will be fraught with changes! I predict that our foreign aid will be cut to a mere dribble for the nations we have helped must start to help themselves!… America has poured billions into the coffers of foreign nations, only to be hated, despised and abhorred!...For the first time in this century America will consider herself first! The key word of America will be "Nationalism."

I predict that Jacqueline Kennedy Onassis will make a very special pilgrimage to Rome in memory of her late husband and brother-in-law...Aristotle Onassis will build a Greek Catholic Church in Athens to perpetuate the memory of his son who recently died...
A famed Senator who recently had a face lift and a body lift will sue his doctor...The Department of Health will be completely renovated by computer. This will weed out frauds and save the Federal Government millions of dollars every day!

Political tipsters will take hard look at George Wallace for place on Democratic ticket in 1972. He is slated to carry five or more states...Rome fashions will produce full-length skirts, 100 percent transparent...Vandalism will sink ships in Pacific and Atlantic...Russia and China will emerge as allies.

I predict that the political kettle will boil over with the force and strength behind Governor George Wallace of Alabama. The Wallace Third Party will be so strong that it will be joined by the Democratic Party and sweep the polls from coast to coast...Unisex clothing (both men and women will be dressed exactly alike) will make great inroads in the fashion world of 1975...Air travel will improve due to the many complaints by customers, as to food, comfort and schedule.

Governor George Wallace of Alabama will hold a worldwide television rally to establish "True Americanism" through his "True Democrats"! This rally will be designed to erase the bad taste many foreign nations have over the Viet Nam "pull out" and the international intrigue which followed!…The Labor Party of England, now under the full influence of Communist influence, will state that "England has one hundred millionaires but also one hundred million beggars!"

Somewhere in the future is a fantastic serum when administered once, need never be given again! This serum is a mono-serum, good for all foreign ailments in the body which it attacks and destroys!…We are moving into an age of computer medicine where diagnosis never change!…I predict that the Governors of many states have been shaken by the attempt on the life of Governor George Wallace and will double their protection around offices and mansions.

I regret to predict that our glorious flag will fly at half-mast on March 31 which will be a day of sadness and loss to us…Regardless of denials, all is not well in Buckingham Palace as the British are restless over the increasing costs of pomp and circumstance, the increasing Irish revolution plus the sliding economy. England is no longer making friends on a world-wide basis, only enemies…There will be another death among the leaders which will stun the world.

I predict that over 10,000 citizens of the upper brackets who paid no income tax or very little, will have their returns examined and be called in for questioning. This will go back to 1968 BN (before Nixon). We can run away but we cannot hide from the IRS…Senator George McGovern will lock up the presidential nomination for the Democratic Party even before balloting…the Black Betterment Society will demand the end of all seniority in business, clubs, brotherhoods and fraternities.

I predict that a new equalizing sales tax on all items will be the next Congressional Plan! A rent tax of 5 per cent will be levied on all rental property, apartments, separate dwellings, motel, hotel and mobile living parks. Auto repair shops will be licensed and each repair will have a price ceiling! You will be able to fly for much less, as airlines will cut frills and give good service for a much lower price. Huge price cuts will come very soon.

I predict a revival of the black arts from Africa…Many spirits of magic witchcraft also crowd the scene, and many cults will be transplanted into our America and will become a vital force in our philosophy…There will be a ''collect before delivery'' enforced on the camp followers who take advantage of a candidate's good credit rating…I predict that Washington, DC will soon whisper that a famed hostess will no longer be welcomed by Democrats nor Republicans due to her vicious gossips and untruths.

I predict a super-confidential double wedding will be held with a top-secret list, when four top western stars of television and motion pictures exchange vows…the greatest smuggling action is not narcotics, jewelry, or contraband, but Bibles—behind the Iron Curtain!…The so-called "Silent Majority" is very much alive. Products are gathering dust on store shelves when the tv-radio personality advertising the item displeases the buyer. Customers will not be forced into submission with unpopular views and philosophies.

I predict a famous senator will slowly drink himself into oblivion. His family and friends, however, will not accept his terminal state in spite of doctors' warnings…a new television series, Horror Movie of the Week, will really entertain you with very new, very fresh and very spooky material…Margaret Truman's book about her father will be a runaway best seller…you will be frisked for a gun, a bomb or a knife on your next plane ride.

I predict that telecasters and broadcasters will be very much disappointed with the ratings on TV and radio as to football, baseball and basketball…Washington whispers that Mamie Eisenhower turned down a proposal of marriage to an old friend of the family…that Reverend Billy Graham may take a six months leave of the pulpit…and that Senator Edward Kennedy faces a revival of popularity with the voters…Senator Goldwater will take a most dramatic stand on the present economic situation and will have many backers.

I predict that the Supreme Court will rule that abortion is murder…A wife aborted a child

which could have inherited great wealth and the husband-father brought murder charges!

This will be the deciding case…There will be revolutionaries at both the Republican and

Democratic conventions this year, and they will be met by force at both…On a quiet and

sedate street in Beverly Hills a great scandal that will rock the nation will take place.

I predict that the next law to be introduced in Congress will be "Nothing But The Truth In

Advertising" and this law will have heavy teeth…A famed Senator will desert his wife and

five children for a Capitol page.

I predict that there will be a cut-back on foreign aid, and no money will be permitted to

leave the borders of America soon. It is time that Uncle Sam quit being Uncle Sap…our

generosity has turned into stupidity…Do not be shocked to witness the return of national

prohibition, slowly but surely 1975 will be a poor year for doctors and undertakers for you

are all too healthy and will live on and on and on…Rockefeller and Reagan will head the

Republican ticket for 1976.

I predict that Jackie Kennedy will again become a bride in 1976 to a former member of her

late husband's Cabinet…that Philadelphia will really be the only city to cash in on the

200th Birthday celebration of our nation, with a carefully planned program which will

excite the world…that a new type of non-chemical face peel will sweep the men and women of the world who seek a new bright happy young face through Beatrice Edwards and her remarkable European-Japanese formula.

I predict that a court fight looms over the will of the late Aristotle Onassis which will shake up both sides of the Atlantic...Penalties for possession, sale or taking of marijuana in Russia, China, India and the Arab nations will be strengthened and the death penalty applied...The news services, TV, radio and the media world have prepared the biographies of ten world famous personalities as they could be that near death!

TRUTH OF THE MATTER: I predict that smoldering scandals of Washington, D. C. will burn holes on the front pages of your favorite newspaper! These documented incidents will all but remove the mantle of greatness from Roosevelt, Truman, Eisenhower, Kennedy, Nixon and Ford! I predict that the Pentagon will soon announce a successful death ray using the laser principle! This potent combination discovered by the Pentagon could make a great change in our military might!

Alice Cooper, the rock star, will marry publicly to a very surprising personality...I regret to predict a tragic scandal in the world of football where there is an actual murder in the shower room after a bitter game and the antagonism of the field is carried into the dressing room...A super lens will be implanted in your ordinary glasses which will give you perfect

20-20 vision without strain or distortion…Detroit faces some stormy weather ahead plus a new crime rise.

I predict that Indira Gandhi will face wrathful voters in the coming elections in India…Coretta King will remarry later this year to a most important Washington figure…Jacqueline Kennedy Onassis will not suffer for lack of friends in her coming criticism of behavior brought on by the jealousy of others…Ladybird Johnson's official autobiography will contain unknown incidents in the life of her famous husband.

I regret to predict that five famous personalities will depart from the land of the living within the next week, and the news of their passing will shock the world…there will be shocking news out of 1600 Pennsylvania Avenue very soon…a strange new bible will soon be published which will clearly degrade mankind and the world…many air fares will be cut to bolster the sagging business of travel. You can expect first class to be abolished and coach service to be brought up to standard.

I predict much bitterness in New York State politics. The Rockefeller vs. Lindsay camps are slowly choosing sides and any day the bitterness will break into the open…I predict that with the increase in crime the motor (murder) cycle will be outlawed by Italy…Vice President Agnew's new biography will be a best seller and will be the most controversial to date...I predict a new fad of Chinese and Oriental food due to President Nixon's visit to China.

I predict that President Nixon will be most triumphant in his coming European tour...one of our most famous politicians, high in political life, will be charged with the murder of his brother...the streets of New York will be cleared of all narcotic pushers, prostitutes, pimps and muggers...the FCC holds seven "stop and desist" orders on seven radio and television stations found guilty of giving only one side of the news...Texas will be plagued with cattle rustlers!

I predict that when the history of the 1900s is written President Johnson and President Nixon will be judged the greatest Democratic and the greatest Republican President we have ever had...I further predict that Mr. Nixon will serve a third term...declining pool room business will be helped by topless waitresses who will shoot you friendly game of pool...Hollywood will uncover a "school" for pickpockets and muggers to train teenagers to feed their drug habits.

I predict that the "Watergate Hearings" will bring wrath upon the heads of senators who cannot afford waves in a coming election year. The reaction is very strong and negative among housewives who resent missing their favorite soap serial, the blood of daytime television...the price of milk will increase despite complaints...the new social registry will be late due to further deletions. A very famed political family will find themselves removed completely.

I predict that a very popular question in the Midwest will be "Is President Nixon being robbed of his civil rights?"…From the South where most elected officials are strong segregationists, the public is amused by their sudden stand in the Watergate affair. Has President Nixon suddenly become the underdog with a national flow of sympathy?…Most American workers are becoming discontented due to the problems of the lunch period.

I predict that an abundance of chicken, turkey, fish and pork will flood the market resulting in rapidly lower prices! Our bumper crop of vegetables and fruit will also have the same effect. The God-made law of supply and demand will take over from man's bumbling handling…I also predict that the aftermath of the Watergate inquiry will be that five famous southern senators will not run for re-election for they have made themselves unpopular with the voters at home.

I regret to predict another Watergate situation out of the deep south which will wreck careers, reputations and fortunes! A political bandwagon will wind up in the gutter, with all politicians feeling the results! There will be three prominent suicides and five out-and-out murders! This festering wound will deeply penetrate America for the next fifty years!

The night is dark, and we are far from home, lead kindly light! This incident will lead us to a national day of prayer!

I predict that some members of the Congressional Watergate Committee will be defeated by their voters in the coming election...Sweden will break with diplomatic relations with America...there will be a new racial crisis in Australia by early spring...Wall Street will hang on the predictions of Jimmie the Greek Snyder of Las Vegas...the death penalty will be revived in 50 states within one year because of the rise of crime, the killing of policemen and the heavy drug traffic.

I predict that the federal laws of copyright will be strengthened and extended to a flat sixty years of protection...Gordon Sinclair of Canada (author of *A Message To Americans*) will have his TV program shown here in America...the Black Betterment will demand a luxury tax on all advertising, black and white, billboard, radio, television plus all newspapers and magazines...many Senators who tried to break the establishment with the Watergate Hearings will succeed in breaking themselves!

You will soon hear the whispers from Washington that three Supreme Court Justices have incurable diseases and will pass this year...Storms on the Atlantic and Gulf of Mexico in late Spring...More damage coming on Pacific coast from small series of quakes...The Bear

(Russia) and the Dragon (China), Nostradamus predicted, will unite and sweep all Asia and Europe before them in 1975.

November 18th will be a day of heartbreak for Buckingham Palace, in which the entire world will join...Howard Hughes will bowl over the imagination and will make Las Vegas the Paris of the West...Alabama faces an industrial boom second to none due to the personal invitation of Governor George Wallace to industries...The stock market will continue to drift upwards...Nixon and Agnew will be reelected.

I predict that Spiro Agnew, our former vice president, will again enter politics, not as the Governor of Maryland but as a Senator!...that San Diego California will face a city political scandal this year, which will become a national matter...that one of our new compact automobiles will be recalled as many accidents and also deaths have resulted among the new owners...that the newest rage in record collections will be those by Hildegarde, with some of them bringing fantastic prices.

I predict that Senator Humphrey and Senator McGovern will make a shocking political deal which will amaze the nation. I had predicted the date of November 18th, 1971, as a most important date, which never happened before!...which would be the devaluation of the American dollar...but I was exactly one month early. The event took place on

December 18th…I can safely predict that the first woman Governor of California will be Shirley Temple Black! Sit back and watch this prediction come to pass.

I predict the rising tide of public opinion will soon question how President Nixon could landslide 48 out of the 50 states and two years later fall into supposed ill repute without being contrived. A thousand men and women will face the charge of treason for manipulating the news, the tide will turn and have 100 percent full American backing by the voters. This drive will be spearheaded by the unions, long maligned…a famed Southern Senator will expire from cancer.

I predict that the average Mr. and Mrs. Voter will turn thumbs down on the question of amnesty. They will take a bitter view and name those seeking amnesty as "traitors"…many hospitals will close due to the falling birth rate and fewer automobile accidents now that speed limits of 55 are in effect…the drama classes of high schools, colleges and universities will tour their productions publicly this coming season.

I predict that the life of Dan Rice, the Civil War Clown who even made Lincoln laugh, will be filmed…the radio serial of days gone by, *One Man's Family*, will soon turn up on TV…western and country music will be the next sensation in music in America…John Wayne will refuse to attend a very liberal political rally…one of our richest cowboy actors will marry an airline hostess soon.

I predict Congress will vote more government interference in business with a new set of edicts this session…the engagement and marriage of Princess Anne will crowd the Irish disaster from the front pages…the Suez, the Panama and the Gibraltar Straits will be bypassed by air power and be only a pride of ownership…Sidney Margolius' paperback *Great American Food Hoax* will draw unusual attention.

I predict that a famed Senator will break his public promise to marry his secretary. A divorce from his legal wife would cost too much…I predict that a Hollywood movie star, wracked with the worry of terminal cancer, will make three quick films for his swan song…I predict that a London medical genius will soon collapse from his increased drug and alcoholic habits.

I predict that a recently released compact automobile will be recalled pronto. The model seems to disintegrate after the first three thousand miles! I predict that Gloria Swanson and Vivian Kellems will win their tax fight on singles…I predict that the widow of Charles DeGaulle will remarry this year I predict that Cuba will offer child brides who are also domestics at a very low price.

Keep your eye on Mayor Sam Yorty of Los Angeles in the New Hampshire primaries for President…I predict Federal Food stamps will no longer be issued to those who buy liquor and drugs from black market sources who face felony charges…One thing the great weathervane of Government shows: war against filling stations which shortchange you on the amount of gas!

Your next radio or TV set will have an informant built-in next year! It is alive and connected with a nerve center of information in Washington; in case of an emergency the announcement will reach you instantly at home, in your office or car…Senator Margaret Chase Smith will be the first woman to be named to the Supreme Court…The "horse fever" epidemic will prove fatal to many men, women and children.

I predict that Chicago's Mayor Daley will prepare a shocking announcement…a senator will be blamed for his wife's death…it will be discovered that the latest bride of a judge neglected to divorce her last husband…the widow of the late Charles DeGaulle will marry a much younger man a new law will go into effect where no one can be refused credit due to color, sex, religion or financial condition…a price war on color TV sets will occur very soon.

I predict that every nation in the world will declare an economic war against America. Uncle Sam has been Good Sam much too long. The American dollar was cut to shreds in foreign trade just for spite…projected gas rationing will result in an abundance and backlog leading up to a price war. The one solution would have been the Alaskan Pipeline but due to the petty politics of the moment we squandered our oil security.

I predict the fiery career of a famed senator will end by death…charges of treason will be placed against ten famous Hollywoodites this month due to their aid and comfort to the enemy…new series of drug problems for the world of education which will stagger under the curse…the end of "junk" mail for no longer can your name and address be sold by one business to another…you (men and women) will soon be out of style if your hair is long.

I regret to predict the suicide of a famed Justice of Washington, DC…There will be a big back-stage battle in the American Medical Assn within the next three months…The Security Exchange Commission will try to trace down the "Witch of Wall Street" who gives out fantastic market tips who will prove to be a famous male astrologer and is highly successful and rich…the bones of 77 skeletons found near Walnut Creek, CA will be from an old Indian Burial Ground.

CRISWELL PREDICTS . . . Roumania will become the first nation to hold a public sex lottery for taxation. This will happen in 1982.

People, Places, Things, & Headlines of the Future!

I predict you will read these headlines in your newspaper during 1975: KING CHARLES III ON BRITISH THRONE...DOW JONES TOPS 1500...RED CHINA PLAGUE SWEEPS ORIENT...DEATH COMES TO THREE SUPREME COURT JUDGES...FRANCE IN NEW TURMOIL...RUSSIA PURGES TEN MILLION TRAITORS...ITALY ENJOYS NEW ECONOMIC BOOM...GERMANY ISSUES NEW WORLD BONDS...CHINA AND RUSSIA SIGN NEW PACT...COMETS TERRIFY BRAZIL

I predict that ratings of movies will be a thing of the past, and many churches, PTA, American Legion and Fraternal groups will plan a 100 percent boycott of poor taste and porno graphic subjects...Walt Disney will plan five family comedies for 1972...I predict it will be the unwritten law that women can carry a gun to protect themselves against all attacks, rape, and purse-snatchings.

PEOPLE...PLACES...THINGS! I predict that Russ Bernhardt will have his 33rd Season in his portrayal of *Scrooge In Person*, the award-winning one-man show, soon to be seen on tour and on your tv screen! This remarkable portrayal will be given a special award by President Ford at a special White House appearance!...I predict that Washington DC will be the first city to have 100 percent Police Protection due to the mounting crime and murders early next year!

Acupuncture will become a part of our lives…vitamin E will gain favor…Los Angeles will face a bitter campaign for Mayor this fall…Thomas Eagleton will return to politics stronger than ever…Roman style togas will be the next topcoat for stylish men…arson will become a major means of protest against the establishment and the perpetrators will meet with many arrests and many convictions.

We cannot invent the future for it is out there waiting to happen! I predict that by June 30, 1977, every man, woman and child will have their finger prints on file in Washington, DC all-in apple-pie order! You will also receive an identification card to carry with you at all times. This will clear out the illegals in our nation, find missing husbands and locate many criminals!

I predict that Television will no longer be that "vast wasteland" but a flowering paradise with the new programs soon to be shown on NBC-CBS-ABC networks!…that the rising death rate of babies, suddenly dying in their cribs, will be the next investigation of the AMA Conference, nationally! Far too many deaths without a clear cause!…I predict that the TV special "Frank and Eleanor" —The Roosevelts— will be tested as a daytime soap opera with all political implications removed!

I predict the following ten headlines will change our world as we know it today! (1) Famine strikes India without reason or mercy. (2) Glacier rolls over northern Alaska. (3) Sea monsters invade the Amazon River. (4) Cannibalism sweeps in a revival in Africa. (5) Bloody elections in Viet Nam. (6) Under-sea volcanoes endanger Japan. (7) British Diplomat assassinated. (8) Strange meteor terrifies South America. (9) Tidal wave sweeps entire coast of Argentina. (10) Life discovered in far off outer space.

Many thousands of doctors will be faced with malpractice suits, in which the victim will collect due to hospital and medical mistakes! The new boost in Hospital costs will bring a new Niagara of public complaints and will result in a Congressional hearing! The farmers of Indiana will copy the fertile way of planting crops of 50 years ago, as the many new ideas fostered by the Agriculture Department for the last 25 years have not been too successful! Soil will get old fashioned home remedies.

I predict that personal survival kits will be the new gift rage, as they contain food and comforts for a ten-day period...just beyond the horizon you will find that the Dow Jones will continue to stay hovering well above the one thousand average...talking magazines and newspapers with musical backgrounds from Japan will prove to be a new novelty...a new type of candy, wholly antiseptic and white in color, will soon hit your candy counter.

I predict that Lee Radziwill will write her autobiography with no punches pulled and will reveal to the world the true Jacqueline Kennedy Onassis...James Stewart will play the title role for tv's "Lindy" based on the life of Col. Charles Lindberg...a most shocking medical announcement will be issued to the effect that marijuana when used by prospective parents can result in the baby born without brain covering, which will never heal over, leaving the child a hopeless vegetable.

I predict changes in England: The dole of welfare will end and be replaced by soup kitchens where the food will have to be cooked and eaten; full wartime restrictions will be in effect. Everybody will be assigned a job; unions will be abolished overnight...The best seller in 1972 will be *The Yellow Emperor's Classic of Internal Medicine*...the supernatural in the concept of disease—the weather and your health!

I predict that Justice will be determined by the computer, fairly. The plain unvarnished truth will come out the plain unvarnished justice!...Just as films and books became raw so they could find buyers, I predict that sports will be brutalized for this very same reason...Ginger Rogers will revive her Charleston dancing days in a nostalgic blaze of glory...France will suffer another national strike which will affect all of Europe and spread to Northern Africa.

The new Holiday Inns will stagger your imagination in elegance and low cost of service...Price war coming soon on light bulbs due to startling discovery to be marketed by the Japanese...Home financing costs will soon drop, starting building boom...IRS computers will scan returns of all doctors, dentists, lawyers for Medicare infractions.

I predict that the Russian author Solzhenitsyn will ask for military protection very soon...that Angela Alioto, wife of San Francisco's Mayor, will prove to be the best vote getter for the next governor of California...Flo Gently, the British singer, will team up with Sweet Afton for the next musical rage, equaling the Andrew Sisters in popularity...Alabama Governor George Wallace will make great political splash with his "True Democrats" and will gain much aid nationwide.

Falling birth rate will result from fewer payments for children of welfare mothers...Even the "incubator" mothers out of Chicago have called a halt to this welfare racket. Supermarkets will be deglamorized, no fancy shelves and no trading stamps, no packing boys (you will do it yourself) and all this will cut food costs about ten percent...You will be shocked when one of our super-stars of sports dies from overdose of drugs while playing...A flood of counterfeit tens and twenties will flood our nation from both Canada and Mexico this winter.

I predict that Anderson, S. C. will be the number one printing city in America with the new contracts from the publishing companies…New York City will suffer a new invasion of sewer rats…San Francisco should beware of a flood of counterfeit currency…Chicago will face a transportation strike…Miami Beach will have a big summer season this year…Paducah, KY area will uncover a nationally important political scandal.

You will have more money to spend in 1971…Federal housing, big dormitories will accommodate thousands…Great advances in medicine coming…Sex will be more than possible after 60, childbirth to 50 and beyond…You will travel more now than at any time in your own lifetime.

Small hospitals which cannot afford to purchase expensive health care equipment will soon be able to lease these medical machines through a Chicago corporation…lovers of nostalgia will rave over the latest version of 1922s musical comedy hit, Irene…millions of Americans will soon again use auctioneers to sell farms, houses, furniture, art and automobiles…the upcoming new look in fashions, the Baby Dumpling look, will be welcome by many women.

You may soon have your own videotape units in your own home for less than $1,500 where you may tape your own TV programs for your own audiences…Russia plans to export her new trucks which we recently helped her to finance and will undercut the Japanese prices…Many housewives will boycott higher prices of foods…Soon Adult education will be furnished free to those who wish to further their profession!…New automated bookkeeping machines will catch many who are taking welfare checks illegally.

Acupuncture will become a part of our lives…vitamin E will gain favor…Los Angeles will face a bitter campaign for Mayor this fall Thomas Eagleton will return to politics stronger than ever…Roman style togas will be the next topcoat for stylish men… arson will become a major means of protest against the establishment and the perpetrators will meet with many arrests and many convictions.

College and universities will no longer have dormitories, but all students will live off campus and come under direct control of city police…A number of clergymen are running for public office and winning…A gaping hole caused by a meteor hitting the South Pacific will be a major marvel of the year…A new safe medicine out of Germany will dissolve fatty tissues in your body overnight.

The next week will be an exciting one for you!…I predict that Las Vegas will reduce prices to tourist level so that a more profitable year ahead can be guaranteed! This will be most welcome for the State of Nevada which depends on the profits from gambling to replace taxes!…I predict that Bette Davis will play the role of Sarah Bernhardt in the coming film "Sarah" which will reveal the truth about this famed actress and pull no punches!

A new crisis will explode between England and Iceland over fishing rights, which will boost prices in our canneries! Diplomatic relations will be severed!...I predict that your personal Tarot Card for the week ahead will be "The Hanged Man" for you are safe from harm or injury, as the Man is hanged by the ankles not the neck! Do not become a martyr so make drastic changes at once! You are resisting your good by pampering your ego and delighting your physical!

I predict that all grade and high school athletics will be discontinued due to the high cost and the dwindling grades of the students...Many high school graduates cannot even spell the names of their city correctly nor fill out a simple check...a ring of eleven-year-old prostitutes will be found to be operating out of Washington, D. C. and bring shame to the nation...the National Council of Sports will rule against any one over 5 feet 11 inches playing basketball next season.

I predict the divided Irish will team up as one and defeat the British at their own game...I predict the courts will be flooded with 18-21 age groups being sued for merchandise, bad debts, hotel bills, clothing, credit card totals, etc! Up to now, if any business man sold to anyone under 21, he could just whistle. But now the 18-21 group is responsible, and an instant adult, and the long-suffering business world can take action...The mounting number of brain tumors cannot be taken lightly. Is there a germ that is breathed in the system which lodges in the brain and causes death?

I predict that a new drug from Japan will soon be introduced which will cure alcoholism once and for all, working wonders on "winos", "beer drunks" and even "brandy hounds"…the next cosmetic sensation will be spray-on wigs for men and women. A one-dollar spray bottle will give you ten different wigs…A new instant developer will give you 8mm movies in your own home in ten seconds…*General Hospital* will win TV's Emmy award as the best serial soap opera of the year.

I predict that the next vacation spot to gain favor will be in Pennsylvania where the green rolling hills will become small estates centered with shopping malls. This historical bit of America will draw many tourists to the triangle section of Harrisburg, Gettysburg and Littlestown and land will skyrocket in value many convicts will shorten their prison terms by volunteering to act as human guinea pigs for the prison doctors.

I predict that insects will grow in size and strength! The common cockroach will triple in size, the Palmetto bugs will grow into mouse size, flies will be able to carry off a cube of sugar from your table and vicious beetles bite hunks out of your skin! No matter what our poisons are against these insects, they will win out!…I predict that property owners in many states will organize a "tax strike" against the new school tax, which is breaking the communities with the frills and fancies!

I predict that future GIs will have their ears pierced so that their "dog tags" may never be lost or stolen…The services offered by a New York company will be stopped by the US mails due to certain fraudulent promises based on giving you sexual power through computers…Smutty dialogs which offend will be edited from future Broadway plays due to the many complaints…The firming of domestic and foreign markets will bring Dow Jones average to 1400 by 1975…South and West will feel the pull first—King Cotton and Queen Oil the reasons.

I predict that we will soon be eating "non-food" pressed from thin air-and it will prove to be most healthy! The compressing cost will be so little, that we will have a bulwark against all of the threats of famine and food shortage!…The fact of rationing is still very much with us. There are those newly elected in Congress, who will move to ration everything but love!…I predict a bumper crop for grain, fruit and vegetables this year, despite all of the unfavorable weather we have had!

I predict that you will soon be able to order your funeral by mail! Your casket will be sent you for easy storage in a closet, a book of instructions what to do when death occurs, plus a full contract with a local mortuary for embalming…many tourists will be caught in South America with a new series of revolutions under the sponsorship of Fidel Castro…many banks and Savings-Loan companies will offer food tickets for new depositors…this will take the place of dishes, radios and books.

I predict that the next house you build will be of steel and glass and a new type of poured concrete. It will have solar heating, sonic cleaning and a vanishing swimming pool…the greatest land boom in American History will soon take place…Ireland and Italy will soon join the inner group of world powers…the changing international scene could create a new series of situations almost overnight…your telephone service will improve with the new automation now being installed on a nationwide basis.

As many as 50 of our present TV shows, I regret to predict, will go off the air…There will soon be a flood of forged diplomas, employers should be on the alert about who they hire…There will be a shortage of pineapple soon because of blight of the crop in Hawaiian crop…An epidemic will strike our shores this summer, bringing swelling of joints gastric condition.

I predict that Queen Elizabeth II will issue her intimate autobiography for the holiday gift buyers this year…that Yadkinville, NC will double its population within the next five years…that vending machine divorces and vending machine marriage licenses will be the next rage out of Mexico…that Sheila Graham will zoom to the top of the best seller list with her fantastic and quite amazingly frank book *A State of Heat.*

I predict that Spain will weather the change in government very well and will emerge as a potent power in Europe and regain the former glory of the past. The Latin world will come into greater position and Spain will have a stronger link with South America!…I predict that the "American" Look will become the fashion of the world in the new Unisex design sponsored by Mr. Blackwell and other famed American designers!

I predict a growing morals scandal between the adults and the members of boy's baseball and football teams which will blow the roof off a Washington, DC area team…the rat population of Montreal will increase with the trouble centering around an abandoned grave yard…You can expect a whiskey price war on bourbon within the next six months due to an over-supply and a decrease of drinking…amateur enthusiasm will revive many community theater projects.

Social security benefits will again be raised ten percent within a year…Next food for diet faddists will be the lowly pear…The finish on a new high-priced automobile peels off when the sun hits it…The new camp trailers will have police looking after them as the latest mode for prostitution on wheels…Las Vegas will be the next major production for film and TV tape.

I predict that Queen Elizabeth II of England will be very busy denying the fact of her failing health, the threatened divorce in the Royal Family and her abdication in favor of her son,

Prince Charles...Rome will be plagued by a new series of art robberies which will equal the British looting of European museums during WWII...Police will use an instant test on the back of the hand which will reveal intoxication and drug intake.

I predict that the Prince of Wales must soon choose a wife so he may be crowned a married king...that the wife of a famed senator refuses to have him buried in a Roman toga as he wishes...that Sonny and Cher, although divorced, will team up again for TV...the IRS will recall the late President Johnson's last three tax statements of income for further investigation.

I predict a film biography of this remarkable faith healer and religionist late in 1976!...That one of our top TV newscasters and commentators will soon announce that he is a "heroin addict" and will try for the cure in Louisville! This household word will shock you when this happens as he has wide acceptance!...That Senator Tunney of California who has Tom Hayden as a contender in the coming election will defend his conservative stand on air command!

I predict that a huge memorial for the late Dictator Mussolini will soon grace the center of Rome...that three Hollywood movie magazines will combine to stay in business, as will three national women's magazines...in the early part of 1975 a new Dictator will arise in Europe Dictator who will be neither communist nor fascist but will please all...a powerful

Arab leader will tour with his harem, opening Las Vegas this October…one out of every ten credit cards could very well be bogus.

I predict a new national service to find your missing wife, husband, son, daughter, sweetheart or friend for only $125 with a refund of $75 if not successful by Teltec of Beverly Hills, Calif. Usually to locate anyone costs you heavily, but this new fantastic method brings results. Many Hollywood professional people use this Teltec, and even they are amazed at the results!…I predict that many thousands of teenagers will take to the road and will live by theft, muggings, and robberies "to call attention to their carnal." desires.

I predict that the World of Sports will make several changes very soon…professional basketball will not permit any player on the court over 5 feet 11 inches tall to standardize the game…football will become "brutalized" to an alarming degree to compete with the excitement of ice hockey and the roller derby…Salmonella, the deadly food poisoning, will appear in the Midwest in canned peaches and pears…there will be a new series of road blocks to stem the growing tide of crime the most innocent looking drivers often carry contraband narcotics!

I predict that the mail delivery will become so uncertain that one of our largest banks will train and use carrier pigeons on an exclusive basis!…A new Cook Book will contain some priceless recipes of Ladybird Johnson, Patricia Nixon and Betty Ford, all family tested for generations!…I predict that long hair will be out of fashion for men and be replaced by the "Gatsby Look" of the 1927-28 era! This is close-cropped, sculptured and smart!

The United States may face one of the most crippling mail strikes in all history! This breakdown in the mail service would paralyze business. I predict that there will be the return of the one cent post card so that more people can be in contact with each other! I predict that free marriage licenses and free divorces will soon be given as a premium in Nevada as a tourist attraction! I predict that a tiny insect in the air when breathed goes into a lung infection and could be fatal to many who have respiratory problems!

I predict that public education will no longer permit useless subjects to be taught and studies will become highly practical…new simple patterns for women's dresses will reduce the cost of a dress to a fraction of present prices…Hollywood faces a bitter, grim strike of writers, technicians, actors and directors which will paralyze television…plant lice will invade the many rose gardens on the west coast.

Food stamps will no longer be issued to persons who buy liquor and drugs from black market sources…Taxpayers will go on a strike in Los Angeles led by Mayor Sam Yorty…There will be a demand made for one black musician to be employed to stand by for every white musician…Millions of bats will invade Baltimore from the sea and bay areas in their search for insects.

All the Super-Markets will be redesigned for the eye-appeal sale to men, and not women! Women compare the values, the weight and the size, while the man just impulsively buys! You will also notice that canned goods will have a very flashy label which is designed to catch the eye of the man! Churches will take an active part in "The-Right-to-Work" revision of laws soon to be in the news! Many church members are "anti-union" due to the limitation they have seen through burials and funeral services with no music permitted graveside!

You will welcome with laughter the TV cafe act of "Fat is Beautiful" girl, Vega Maddux …the widow of Charles DeGaulle will tell all in a new biography…Franco of Spain will abdicate in favor of Prince Jean by late summer…Governor George Wallace, of Alabama, will have a one-hour TV-special on his personal life…The weather this summer will be fantastic, and you and I will be very happy to see the summer over.

Many thousands of doctors will be faced with malpractice suits, in which the victim will collect due to hospital and medical mistakes! The new boost in Hospital costs will bring a new Niagara of public complaints and will result in a Congressional hearing!…The farmers of Indiana will copy the fertile way of planting crops of 50 years ago, as the many new ideas fostered by the Agriculture Department for the last 25 years have not been too successful! Soil will get old fashioned home remedies.

Sweden will not be a tourist favorite this summer, due to the new tourist dollar exchange and the way they are plagued by USA draft dodgers who sought asylum there...I predict that the fad of heart transplants is at an end...A new federal ruling will make doctors responsible for the wrong diagnosis.

I predict that all adoption papers will be opened for protection of the new parents and the identity fully known for later protection of the children...all doctors must make house calls when summoned, and if they refuse their medical license will be withheld when a complaint is made against them as a feature of the new Medicare...congressmen will suddenly take the middle-of-the-road position and veer away from the left on the generosity of welfare because fraud is so widespread.

Prediction! Next year no diplomas will be given unless (1) the student can write (2) the student can read and (3) do simple arithmetic! College entrance exams can be passed by a sixth-grade student so that Minorities will not be discriminated against! The Education Field will have a complete overhauling...I predict that India will collapse from within! Indira Gandhi, the number one woman of Destiny, now ruling India with an iron fist and not even wrapped in a velvet glove, will bring Asia to its feet! Or to its knees!

What is the matter with reading, writing and arithmetic? When a high school graduate cannot make the proper change of a dollar, write out a simple check or read a street map, something must be wrong!…I predict a fantastic year ahead for vacations with the airlines, railways and busses cutting travel prices! Why stay home this summer? Go-go-go!

I predict that bogus theatrical agents will tour the nation offering to represent many children if they have a new series of photographs taken which costs $60, which they split with the local photographer or have one of their own! This is an outright gyp of the first water, so beware of this fraud!…I predict a battle royal behind the doors of Congress over the new demands by Minorities, Inc. for a 10 percent tax on all advertising on radio, television, newspapers, magazines and billboards!

I predict that for a romp in the impossible realms of reality, you must see *The Land That Time Forgot* from the novel of Edgar Rice Burroughs, who gave us Tarzan and the Mars series. It is a beautiful and wayward adventure which will take you back to your youth!…I predict one of the most exciting personalities of this year will be a woman from Paducah, Kentucky, now over 90, but talks on a toy telephone to President Lincoln, and repeats amazing predictions she claims he gives her.

HEADLINES OF THE FUTURE: "Chaos flares in Suez!"…"China and Russia sign new trade pact!"…"England devaluates pound sterling!"…"Hollywood star suicide over fading career!"…"Price war on funerals!"

I predict that a price war on air travel is very much expected, not only for domestic but also for foreign travel!...A new boom of prosperity will strike Alaska other than the pipe line promotion, and this will be mining and ice-fishing!...Many parts of USA will soon face danger of malaria epidemic...New earthquakes strike Canada and Alaska soon...Bell bottom slacks, long hair and leather fringes be dead as dodo by end 1970.

I predict a drive will start to permit faith healers to operate under Medicare and Medicaid! Many citizens will complain but many are healed by faith (and will testify) over the effects of medicine! This will be the next controversy to sweep the nation!...I predict that the natives of Florida will scurry around and prepare themselves for the largest and most profitable season of tourist to date! You Floridians will be most polite to the Yankees, smile and be friendly, for it will pay off handsomely!

I predict that Canada can expect stormy weather...winds, rains, floods, blizzards, avalanches and record snow falls will plague the Canadian areas...one of our largest dog food companies will issue registration papers making every dog a pedigreed dog even though the parenthood was careless...a lazer beam will be used to perform internal operations without cutting the outside flesh and protect the body from aging...the greatest drive on the drug curse yet will soon begin.

I predict that at high noon on a day very soon you will find that one of our largest and richest unions will suddenly decide to fold due to inner-conflict and the withholding of union fees by the membership; the new "billeting law" which permits any color, creed or religion to elect private family, where they will move in and be protected by the Government's new non-discrimination rule which many organizations are now trying to make a law overnight.

I predict that rural and suburban America will no longer pity the city! They have drained their treasuries to aid the city! The city has drawn from the rural who move there for the very sake of welfare! No taxes are paid and they become a cancer on the economic picture. Had they stayed where there was employment and not sought the security of welfare and charity, cities like New York, Cleveland, Chicago, Detroit, Philadelphia and St. Louis would be profitable and economically healthy!

I predict that all American citizens will be forced into good health by diet and exercise, the outlawing of over eating, drugs and alcohol, and mono-serum shots for disease protection…our public school system will be revamped, stressing practical subjects even in elementary classes, schools will operate on a 12-month basis and the cost of education will fall by lowering teacher salaries due to an over-supply of teachers.

Banner headlines will soon inform you that Football, Basketball and Baseball will slowly go broke! The falling box office attendance, the cost in television and radio performance rights plus the repair of many stadiums and on top of this the exorbitant salaries of the players, will bring bankrupt conditions soon to this profession! The general public has no sympathy when the players go out on strike for more money.

I predict that we face a revival of social dancing in our present trend of nostalgia...the residents of Toronto Canada will regret liberalizing their residential zoning as slums will soon follow...from the California fashion world: Pants and slacks for women will be definitely out and a totally unmannish ultra feminine look will be "in"...if you attend a football game in a large city you will be searched for guns, knives and blackjacks, to prevent poor losers from hurting others.

I predict that all insurance on life, collision and damage will be cancelled on all motorcycle riders...that Wall Street will issue a directive on crime which will be watched by all law enforcement departments...that you will soon enjoy the return of the big bands of the 1930's and 1940's...that Juan Peron, who has returned to Argentina after years of forced exile, will appear at a special memorial mass for his late wife, Evita Peron.

I predict that a toy gun set will be taken from the market…It will actually kill a child! It first sends a tracer bullet and then a hard-nosed bullet which can penetrate the skin fatally. This was not an imported toy, but one made by American manufacturers…

I predict that salmonella and ptomaine will romp through the Holiday fruit cake industry, so be very careful! If you notice mold around the fruit embedded in the dough, this could be the tell-tale sign!

Sexxx, Nudism, UFOs, and Outer Space

America's 200th birthday in 1976 will be celebrated throughout space as we will beam this tribute to every corner of the universe…France will soon class marijuana as punishable with death upon conviction of possession or smoking…one of our largest charity organizations will be found to be fraudulent and will be stopped by the Postal Authorities from using the mails to collect donations…the Florida Chamber of Commerce will be most successful in closing many of the tourist traps in their state.

We are entering the "twilight of sin"—due to our ultra-liberal thinking…Once abortion, pornography and open sex acts were outlawed and punishable by jail and fines...In the ultra-liberal world of tomorrow some believe "there will be no sin!"…I predict that the answer to cancer will be found in diet and the diet alone...We are all eating some item that results in cancer in some people…We are what we eat!…I predict a new surge of tourists will sweep down to Florida.

I predict that Howard Hughes will introduce the most sensational innovation in outer space by June 1 and it will take your breath away…You can expect a bitter backstage battle in Wall Street over foreign investments and stocks and bonds which are worthless…Nothing would please some of our lawmakers more than having another Wall Street Crash and I predict that the very liberal Congress will open the floodgates for foreign merchandise of all kinds which will destroy the American products market.

I predict that a new type of computer will measure sexual powers…our Armed Forces will pierce the ear and insert a tiny dog tag for identification…candidates of future election campaigns will have facelifts, hair-transplants and body operations to make them more attractive to voters…more and more American students, traveling in foreign countries, will find themselves in jails on drug and other charges where 50,000 young Americans are already behind bars.

I predict that the advance weather report for outer space in the vicinity of Mars and Venus will be winds of a million miles per hour…This could endanger our exploration into space. We know nothing of the dangers of outer space…The Federal Communications Commission will demand that "news" remain news, not supposedly satiric comments and laughter by the newscaster. They will rule that "freedom of speech" does not include the distortion of the facts.

Smaller towns will have more banks, as people demand more personalized banking service…There will be over supply of teachers by end of 1971 due to TV…Flood of non-fiction books coming…Motion picture stars who did permit nudity in their films will find public opinion turning against them by boycotts at the box office.

I predict that our next concern will be bonfires in outer space to plague our astronomers and make it difficult to chart outer space flights. Are they planets shot down by a warlike enemy giving us all warnings?...In the coming election Blacks will vote for Blacks solidly and surely! This will be true in the North and the South, and a Black Empire within America can be built with black votes.

I predict that the nude films have run their course and the family type movie will again be the favorite...one of our richest cowboy actors will marry an airline hostess soon...a famous glamour girl whose drug dosage has so increased that doctors marvel she is still alive will expire...Joey Bishop will soon return to TV with a new guest format...Confidential Magazine will re-appear with many famous writers contributing to its success.

I predict that when the comet Kohoutek leaves our starry heavens, seven world famous personalities will leave the world with it...the nine-year-old daughter of a famed liberal editor will not survive her recent bout with heroin...a very famous athlete will be murdered in the shower room after a successful game...a Southern senator will come to grief due to remarks made on national television...there is talk in his state of lynching after his recall.

I predict the walls of eternity are crumbling: the next theory behind flying saucers will be that they are chariots from the wide blue yonder which will bring the dead back to planet earth...A very dangerous practice (the painting of the face and neck with a light shellac to gain a more youthful appearance) will be outlawed by Pure Food and Drug rulings...the much advertised romance of the ages in Hollywood will burst into explosion with all of the dirty linen being washed in public.

I predict that transparent bathing suits for both men and women will be the rage on public beaches this year...Paris will fade as the style center for the world and be replaced by Hollywood...New York City will double its police force due to the mounting crime in the streets...Air lines will make you a special excursion if you wish to visit the place of your birth this summer, no matter where...A famous glamour girl will be forced to marry her supposed husband before they divorce for the coming settlement.

Oxygen and hydrogen have been discovered on other planets so that means life!...I predict that pierced ears for men will be the latest from London, so that personalized jewelry can be worn with a flair...I predict that you will hear whispers from Washington...A very famous Ex-Governor has turned alcoholic and still acts as if still Governor...Ice blue will be the leading color for summer with silver or gold edging.

I predict a big scandal due to the advertised "sex-change" for $100. Many deaths have taken place after these attempts in the San Diego area...the new "head-start" classes will paint from live nude models...mobile home living will grow by leaps and bounds...in the

Southwest a Niagara of letters will flood congress against any amnesty proposal…lavish musical westerns will return to the motion picture screens of America with great success.

I predict it will be revealed that on our last moon jaunt, mysterious signals were flashed from outer space which suddenly became nearby space. Our scientists will agree that this could readily be a sign that other worlds are watching.

To increase interest in a coming film out of Russia, the Producer will offer the star as a first prize in a sex lottery…A new vitamin from Japan, will be known as the "honeymoon vitamin-mineral" to keep the body toned to a high existence…Crime will so increase that road blocks outside Washington will stop and search all cars before they are permitted to enter D. C.

You must beware of adrosil—"adrosil" is a drug which taken like aspirin controls the senses and demands that you disrobe, even on a busy street or a hotel lobby. This new drug is a potent stimulant which demands that the pores breathe and is even more powerful than the legendary "Spanish Fly"!

I predict paste on bikinis for girls, and clamp on bikinis for men…I predict that a set of septuplets, all boys, will be born in Grand Rapids, La., on January 19, 1973, and all will live—the first such case in history…I predict that the only war ever to be fought on

American soil will be in Alaska in the late 1980's...a combine of Russian, Chinese and Korean forces will try to gain a foothold on North America by bombing the U. S. and then invading Alaska. That state will be virtually destroyed in the fighting.

I predict that an Anti-Discrimination law, permitting members of the same sex to marry will soon have Hollywood caterers featuring wedding cakes with two grooms, or two brides...I predict that Barbara Hutton will soon abound in her 8th marriage...That open fire—open cremation for a new interest in the department of death...That a shocking film will concern Sherman's march to the sea, with all the forbidden truth to be shown.

I predict a growing fad in India will show any political candidate in the nude, as they feel they must not hide anything from the public...you can expect a new wave of kidnappings as ransom seems to be so easy to collect. No great anti-kidnapping laws will be passed until a member of Congress is snatched...a startling innovation in the world of music will be harp music in swing style.

It will be possible to experience intercourse over the telephone and a female can become pregnant from miles away...the Paris keyword for style next year will be feathers made of plastic and imported from Japan...The ecologists have made feathers from living birds suddenly out of fashion to the womenfolk!...It will be possible to send water to the moon through the laser beam.

I predict that Canadian television stations along our border will soon show pornographic films from midnight to 6:00 AM...St. Louis will soon rid its water front along the Mississippi of narcotic pushers and dealers...Pennsylvania police will report more property lost through looting than actual flood damage...a new medical breakthrough (using laser beams) in the study of mental illness.

I predict a famed sports star, whose name is a household word, will fall from grace through narcotics, a shocking sex change and "throwing" the game for a money cut...that you will be able to call the White House on the Nixon Red Telephone to report any overcharges on food, clothing, merchandise, interest and late charge...prostitution will be recognized as a profession in Sweden and unemployment benefits will be granted.

I predict many massage parlors will continue in business under the license of Sex Therapy Centers, although no girl under 14 may be employed...that acupuncture will grow in favor despite the objection of the AMA and will be practiced in some of our larger hospitals before the year is over...the biggest battle of principle will be the permitting of prayer back into the public schools...here is true liberty and freedom of thought promised by the Constitution.

I predict something new in correspondence courses—Sex Education! All problems, personal and impersonal are openly discussed. It will blast the ignorance and innocence about sex…Nostradamus in 1531 predicted "The Men of the Cross" would enjoin the Orange and drive the crown forever from Erwin (Ireland)…This remarkable prediction is happening now, today!

I predict a new type of laser ray which can dissolve the sex functioning organs forever and a day! This dissolves the tissue and no power remains! It is painless and the patient is not told of the simple manipulation!…I predict that a potent gas will be used in germ warfare so deadly that it effects the body instantly, and within hours the gas seeps through every pore of the body and renders it useless! This new gas could advance the science of war a century overnight.

I predict that there is a counter balance to be found for our ills! No disease can exist without a cure, and somewhere out there is a is a simple cure for cancer, arthritis, gout and the common cold!…I predict you will wear plastic lace dresses and suits which will be semitransparent and cut to make you look thinner.

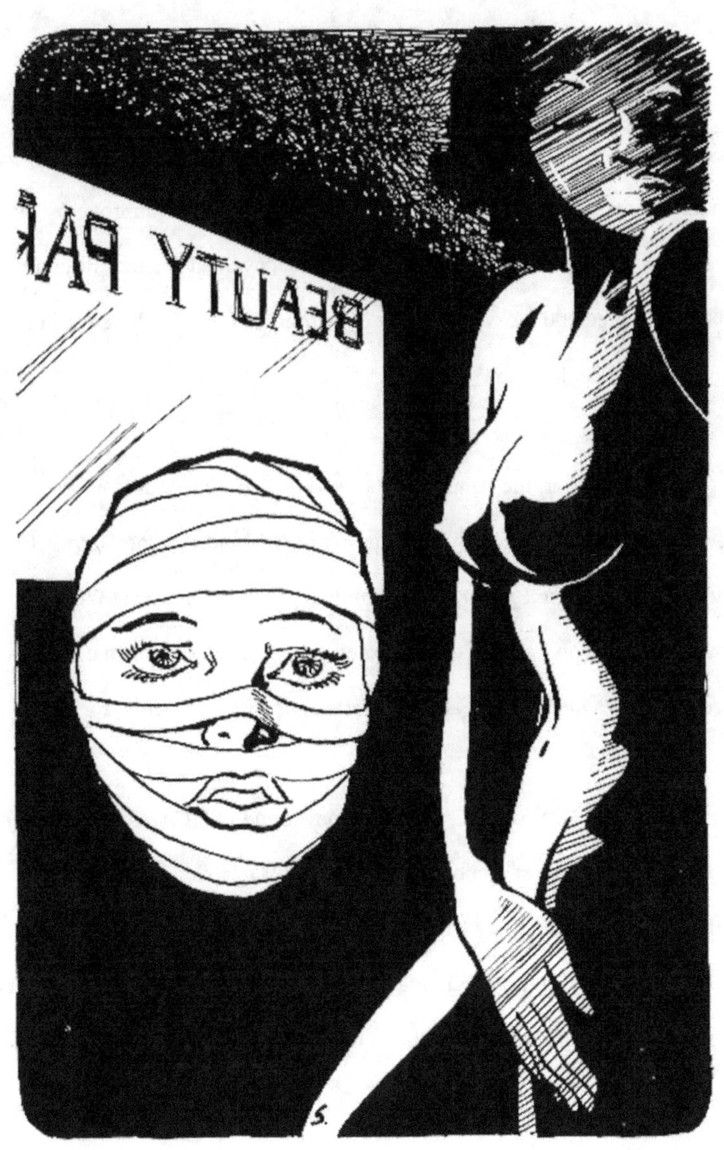

BEAUTY PA

Ghosts of Hollywood

I predict that the ghosts of Hollywood will again be most active in 1972…Life will be discovered on nearby planets…I predict our postal service will improve by dismissal of many postal employees who have been found inadequate, discourteous and unacceptable…I predict there will be terror by twilight in China as the greatest blood purge of all times takes Place!

I predict Josephine Baker, the American star who had all Europe at her feet for years will have her own line of cosmetics and perfumes…Lloyd Lindroth, the Harpist Bazaar, will score the new film *I Woke Up Early* for Columbia, the new Edward D Wood film…Maria Graciette, the Hollywood astrologer, will soon have a handbook for the stars, for instant reference…John Wayne will appear in *Racket Buster* a new departure for him.

I predict that Edward D. Wood Jr. will start a new trend of "Classic Terror" films out of Hollywood utilizing the best combined movie and TV technics plus a new type of horror makeup! You will be able to buy frightening images of James Moore, Valda Hansen, Paul Marco, Harvey Dunn, Mona McKinnon and Jennie Stevens dressed as they were in the films! This new merchandising method will revolutionize the Hollywood scene overnight!

The next authentic ghost story out of Hollywood will be the Paul Marco production of *Some Body Walked Over My Grave*! I predict that the new Political Party in America, the Third Party, will be the Black Party! The Black Party for Black Voters! It will be the most potent party in America in a few short years! The latest fashion fad for men will be shawls! Of all materials! Worn at all times! For any event! You will also be able to get a matching shawl for the girl friend or wife!

I predict that *Tapestry in Terror* starring Vampira and myself will soon be seen as an hour TV program in September of 1971, so watch for it. This is based on *The Night People* by Edward D. Wood. The soundtrack will also be available on an LP album!...The body of Judy Garland will be brought back to Hollywood...Nixon will appoint three judges to the Supreme Court in 1971...Free public medicine is coming in three years...Roy Rogers and Dale Evans in a super-western will make box office cash registers ring.

Roy Rogers and Dale Evans: your international tour is assured...I predict a new series of earthquakes and undersea volcanoes in the Mid-Pacific before the end of this year...I predict that all traffic coming from Mexico and Canada will be treated to a new radaric electric eye which can detect heroin, etc and other drugs instantly. This will sound the death knell to many narcotic smugglers.

I predict that tourists will report seeing the ghost of Clara Bow at high noon standing by her footprints Grauman's Chinese Theater...that the death rate from drownings will be much greater than ever before...that Texas will be the first state to limit population and tourists as too many just stay on for welfare...that a new type of headache medicine will have a built-in vitamin.

I predict the next Hollywood scandal to break publicly will be the secret death and burial of a comedian's wife...a famed talent school, purchased after the death of the founder a few months ago, will be found to be a front for prostitution and narcotics...when all office holders are required to post their income tax statements for the past three years, many will resign to keep from facing a jail sentence!

Many tourists report seeing ghosts of famous movie stars around noon in forecourt of Grauman Chinese Theatre...Canada and Sweden will deport thousands of young men back to USA because they fled to escape the draft...There is a deadly combination of three famous remedies, when taken together, will send your mind to oblivion; it is so deadly it dries out the brain.

I predict that one of our most famous citizens of Hollywood will become a vegetable through the increased use of drugs and alcohol!...We are fast approaching a limitation of free speech! No longer can we have cigarette advertising on the radio and television!

Audible prayer is banned in schools! The libel laws are easily enforced and damages can be easily collected! We must be careful what we say, what we write or the way we act for someone someplace may take offense!…I predict the fast shifting of the inner earth during the 1970s.

The ghost of Marilyn Monroe has driven renters from her former home in Hollywood…Billy Graham will have his life filmed by Hollywood with Charlton Heston…A famous actor will undergo a sex change and do a sister act with his sister…An entire Russian ballet troupe defected to become US citizens…I predict that many residents in Los Angeles will report seeing the spirit of the late Aimee Semple McPherson!

Hollywood Boulevard will become haunted again by the ghost of Marilyn Monroe…I predict one of the untold stories of recent tornadoes will be the uncovering of a cemetery, scattering the caskets and bodies over an unfortunate town…a bill will be introduced in Congress which will automatically extend their present term which will save many officials from the voter's gallows…there will be a new federal ruling where a lawyer must serve a client for a stipulated amount and the legal professional fee will be fixed.

I predict that the Norman Mailer *Marilyn Monroe* will be up for some heavy criticism…many men prisoners strongly object to their jails becoming co-educational…the planned super-film based on the "Lusitania" will not be made because of political implications…hitchhiking will be classed as a felony on a federal basis…many nations of the Middle East will demand that all citizens must marry and have a legal mate.

Tiny Tim will make a spectacular comeback. He will have a new image and nostalgia music!…I predict that the mysterious death of a Cardinal will stir up much anti-religious feeling all over the world!…The month of August may prove to be a perilous one offshore on both the Atlantic and Pacific Coasts! Our geologists warn of another era of undersea volcanoes…All is not lost in Cambodia, for out of this tangled diplomatic mess will come a clear policy for America—no more foreign aid to anyone.

I predict that the next big Hollywood gossip story will concern a former glamour girl's sleeping pill kick as she mourns over an imaginary husband…the bitter humor of Mother Nature will give our world a toss and tumble on Sept. 27, 1973. The time will come when the birth of a baby will be so rare that it will be televised all over the world, due to the pill, abortions, etc… amnesty will never be granted the 250,000 who left our country to avoid serving in Vietnam.

Amos and Andy will return to radio next season…Rampant cannibalism will be next problem of Mid-Africa…Millions of fish will die on beaches of Fla and Cal because of water pollution by human sewage…I predict that Mae West will do her famous Broadway hit *Sextette* in wide screen color for 20th Century-Fox!

I predict that Dinah Shore will soon have her frozen recipes in your favorite supermarket ...Barbara Stanwyck will play the life of Elizabeth Arden, the cosmetic queen, in a new TV series...Bing Crosby and Bob Hope will revive the good old days of vaudeville at the Palace. James Stewart will fore sake his TV role for a love sick professor who instructs senior citizens...Mae West will film *Catherine Was Great* in London, based on her famous stage success of the same name.

Mae West will be the first star to enjoy a film festival from Monday through Friday on national television at prime time...I predict that the welfare dollar will be spent more wisely in the future. Each case will be examined by an unemotional computer and the cheaters cut off from the welfare dollar. Thousands will be jailed. Many are receiving checks in five names!...Florida will surpass California in the shipping of citrus fruits...many automobile owners may expect an annual checkup by the state next year.

The South Seas will open new doors for Americans who will move there in increasing numbers...Our interests will capture the last known Paradise of the world by the end of by 1972...Judy Conova will return in as the corn pone queen in August...The film classic *Birth of a Nation* will be remade...One of our famed universities will ban the long-haired hippy look.

I predict that a huge front-page scandal will grow out of a recent Hollywood suicide...London will crack down on all prostitutes and will control them by a daily collection of taxes...Danger has arisen in the Chicago airport due to lurking muggers who attack and rob persons even in broad daylight...Judy Canova will do a hillbilly version of *My Fair Lady* next season...John Barrymore Jr will appear in a concert version of his father's greatest role, *Hamlet*.

I predict that Judy Canova will have a great new TV series based on her own career...that Mae West will soon issue another book...that three big conventions in Las Vegas will have more in attendance than live in the state of Maine...that death will strike the Royal House of Windsor...that the Irish will protest through the U.N. the strong-arm methods of the English Militia.

I predict that the new Judy Canova *Country Cooking* will delight you with the Midwest recipes of yesteryear! This book should be called "Food To Catch Men By" for it is truly a masterpiece and a gourmet's delight! That a man claiming to be a relative of the late President Calvin Coolidge passing many checks on unsuspecting banks and stores. He speaks five languages fluently and has a charming manner which captivates!

I predict that a famous Hollywood star will commit suicide when told he has incurable cancer...we will continue to have an uneasy peace...very famous doctor will be held on the charge of murder by abortion...there will be a TV spectacular concerning the events of today and narrated by President Nixon...Prince Charles will become King Charles III within this year...former Senator Margaret Chase Smith will return to Washington for a high government post.

The wraith of Walter Winchell has been reported in various places...He appears (ghost) very strong and energetic, very much like he was before his final illness...I predict the Berlin wall will be re-enforced due to the many who escape Red domination...There will be a crippling strike in Paris, at the very peak of the tourist season...This will bring a new national crisis...Canada will soon embark on a program of price fixing...It will even include prostitution among other professional fees.

I predict that the ghosts of Hedda Hopper and Louella Parsons will be seen again in Grauman's Chinese Theater...that scented food will result in a body aroma which will last for 24 hours...that a new Hollywood film based on the Russian practice of drugging children so that they produce babies at the age of ten will shock you...John Wayne will refuse to attend a very liberal political rally.

A return to gracious living which has caught Hollywood prepared with the splashy "1928" Restaurant and Antique Shop! Bric-a-brac! Tiffany lamps! Plants and greenery! Floral wallpaper! With roses as big as cabbages! Together with midwestern cooking served family style!…"1928" will be duplicated in many, many places!…Your Tarot Card for the coming week will be the Page of Swords, signifying you will welcome a younger person into your life!

I predict that hauntings in Hollywood will soon hit your newspaper's front page. Many will report seeing Tom Mix riding high and handsome on his ever-faithful horse, Tony, down Sunset Boulevard…I predict complete computer health diagnosis. After you are examined by walking between the two eyes of the camera lens, the computer will prescribe proper medication, even needed vitamins…I predict all English prostitutes will soon be licensed and unionized.

I predict that a famed Hollywood star will sue a famed doctor for malpractice as he has been treating her shoulder for arthritis and all the time it was broken in three places, giving her great pain and discomfort! Carnage in South Africa! A million lives will be lost for diamonds, gold and radium! Human greed will overcome human kindness in this coming cyclone of death and destruction! Ireland, India and Southern Africa were not corrupted overnight, but with centuries of careful deceitful politics!

I predict a new trek to see the fatal automobile once belonging to Bonnie and Clyde will prove a welcome experience in nostalgia to the world weary…that a viewer-listener boycott of many personalities who have displeased them by their radical views and anti-religious attitudes and expressions and many commentators and newscasters will leave the air later this year…there will be a new mini-TV set which can be strapped to the wrist to be used in crime detection.

The latest Hollywood scandal will center around a five-times married man and his five living ex-wives living harem style in Beverly Hills…I predict that birth control pills will be substituted with codeine for a deadly narcotic mixture which will result in many deaths…I predict a series of non-scheduled flights to Paris and return for only $9.

I predict that Glenn Campbell's change of singing style will gain him a much larger and acceptable audience…The Hall of Mirrors in Versailles will again be in the parade of history, when a top summit meeting is held later this year with President Nixon and all other world leaders…Canada and Sweden will donate thousands of dollars for the "Amnesty Drive" to rid their nations of the draft evaders they had welcomed in the last ten years.

I predict that Zsa Zsa Gabor will wed English nobility…that Queen Elizabeth II will issue her annual "no longer welcome" guest list for the coming social season and many names will amaze you…the recently widowed Duchess of Windsor will visit her hometown of Baltimore very soon…there will soon be an oversupply of teachers due to instruction by television...Doris Day will be awarded the President's Medal for her unselfish work for pets.

Robert Redford, the Great Gatsby himself, will make a surprising confession within thirty days...Milton Berle's new TV series will deal with a backstage romance based on an actual event of some years ago...Rona Barrett will tell all in her coming autobiography, and I do mean all...A new script, recently located among the effects of the late Sir Noel Coward, will prove to be of a great interest to television viewers, as it concerns the many intricate difficult troubles of backstage.

Milton Berle's new routine about our first woman president will make the TV world hysterical...Jimmy Durante: Your life will become a Broadway musical with your old partners Clayton and Jackson...Coretta King: You will be the first woman member of the Black Congress to be held in Africa in November and be hailed as the Black Joan of Arc...In a 90-day period 100,000 families came to California and all applied for welfare the day they arrived.

Marty Allen ("Hellow Dere!") will emerge as a comic genius of our times...A postage stamp will be issued soon in honor of Jimmy Durante and his eternal humor. England will soon have a new ruler Charles III...Ethel Merman will outreach her present fame in a sparkling new musical...Beware of dubious oil venture advertised out of South America

…Three famous Hollywood couples will soon wash their dirty linen in court with hundreds of names…Nader will ride pills, rest homes, hospitals, ambulances and whole medical world!

I predict that the musical life of Jimmy Durante on Broadway, called "Jimmy," with Durante himself in the leading role will break all box office records…I predict that Vice-President Agnew will win the Nobel Peace Prize…The Duke of Windsor wishes to be buried beside his Baltimore bride here in America…The widow of General Charles DeGaulle will marry again shortly after the first of the year.

Hollywood will have a new fad, the seance will replace the cocktail party…Famed star there is still supporting her five husbands in her fabulous mansion which she received from them and in perfect accord and happiness…Over a thousand Hippies are turned back at the Mexican border and refused entrance daily…Son of a famed actor ran away with his new stepmother and actor threatens to shoot both of them on sight.

I predict the so-called "Bible Belt" will speak loud and long in this coming election…Irene Ryan, the granny of Beverly Hillbillies TV fame will electrify Broadway in her new musical…crime now rampant on New York streets will soon feel the strong arm of the law through the new vagrancy rulings by the Supreme Court…that Athens will plan a cultural fair marking 2,000 years of recorded history…that Tunis will prove very unpopular to tourists due to relaxed border restrictions.

A new drive will be started by the Consumer's Institute to guarantee that you receive the amount of gasoline you purchase from the pumps…Howard Hughes will make an appearance much to every one's amazement…Police will suddenly close several communes for being a nest of crime with many arrests and convictions from the so-called "Hippy" population…Queen Elizabeth II will face the wrath of the House of Lords and the House of Commons over her new demands to increase the pomp and ceremony expenses.

I predict an open law suit in Hollywood will soon reveal a well-kept secret! A highly publicized actress who had injections of silicone for facial, bust, hips and buttocks will sue the hospitals for untold damages as her system rejects the silicone as a foreign substance. Usually many tests are taken, and just as a transplanted heart is not successful, the silicone is also rejected by Mother Nature!

A famed TV Movie star widower will be arrested and convicted of having three children by his own three daughters…a new imported face cream will eat holes in your face…the new Nixon Health Plan will make Free Public Health to everyone without fees and doctors will be forbidden to have private practice…more campus violence and crime in the streets.

I predict that in Hollywood the problem of marijuana and stronger drugs will become so great on the sets that the Narcotic Squad will be assigned by the Federal Government, not only for the crew, actors, writers, directors and producers but the name stars will be involved...you will see shocking headlines to this effect...the California Marina will be taken over by water rustlers and it will soon pay all boat owners to have someone on board each hour out of the twenty-four!

I predict that the theft of the body of a famed comic from his casket will be hushed up unless there is a lawsuit over his vast estate...a very famous glamour girl who suffers from a mental illness will be closely watched as she threatens to kill her three ex-husbands, who, she claims caused her unhappiness...there will be a continuous change in our coastal areas where the multiplying underseas and offshore volcanoes do much to disrupt boundary lines.

A television producer rented out his malformed baby to a carnival sideshow...Western music will soon overtake rock and roll, now on its way out...Sexy movies will be a thing of the past, with about 500 unreleased on the Hollywood shelves...Flood of counterfeit money pouring in from Canada, so examine your currency carefully, and if in doubt notify the police...Portable air-conditioners will be the No. 1 export from Japan next summer.

A famed Hollywood star, twice the age of his latest bride will face a damaging lawsuit on a bigamy charge...Silent movies from yesteryear will become a national craze...One of the big band leaders will not last out his tour…The day will come when you will not only

eat the food on your plate but the utensils as well…Soon we can discard and waste

nothing.

For Women Only!

Miracle of 1971: a new type of vitamin will be discovered against all of the minor diseases and common colds…Draft of unmarried men is certain…Tax on bachelors coming…Men will throw themselves at you girls…Milady's fashions go back to 1907, flowery hats, skirts that touch the floor but they will be transparent…Paris will decree it.

I predict that June Wilkinson, the Hollywood personality, will create a new image as an actress, which will be copied for years, as she will set an endless trend you girls will unconsciously imitate.

I predict that in 1972 science will march ahead with a most amazing invention for childbirth which is painless, speedy and safe! The item is the size of a transistor with a cap that fits over the head, giving wild electronic shocks, which dulls the pain, hastens muscular action…a complete do-it-yourself kit for all women! Over a thousand citizens of Ireland will secretly embark for New York to raise money for free Ireland from the Crown. They will be successful!

Q: Will there be a race of super-men?

A: I predict there will be a planned breeding of super-men through artificial insemination now being planned by the United Nations for future generations! Here is a hush-hush prediction: I predict that through the right channels any girl or woman may purchase the sperm of a famous movie or tv star for artificial insemination by her own doctor in her home!

I predict women will gain more in independence in 1975 than any year so far…the bride of the year will be Gloria Swanson who will marry her richest and youngest to date on television…Hale Smith, the champion hiker, will walk from Tijuana, Mexico to Vancouver, Canada protesting pornography…Russian and Chinese submarines will be noticed both in the Pacific and the Atlantic coasts of our nation soon…Mail delivery will be 100 percent improved by a new method soon to be introduced by our Post Office.

Just as women were formerly sold into "bondage", the time will come when men will be sold, about time for fair play!…A famous singer was stricken with cancer of the throat three years ago and since that time a "double" has been recording, upon the singer's death the secret will be known…Janet Gaynor will be seen on the TV screen in the role of an aging Empress in a new historical series!…Wesley Eure who delights adults in *Days Of Our Lives* and every child in *Land of the Lost* from a soap serial star to an adventure star with amazing ease! I predict that from now on out Wesley Eure will be known by just the one name "Wesley" joining Hildegard, Liberace, Fabian and others!

I predict the next Beauty Contest will be for women over 75 which will draw world-wide attention. You will marvel at the beauty of these women…a series of records will be issued on charm and personality for women who want to attract men and for men who want to attract women. These how-to recordings will be the best yet…chemosurgery (the lifting of faces through chemicals) will be perfected in a startling new development to be announced soon.

I predict that a very glamorous star secretly left her entire wardrobe to one of our most famous female impersonators…I predict good news for all women: (1) You will soon have a federally sponsored "Cosmetic Cafeteria" where you may receive free any type of cosmetic of your choice. (2) You may attend bar, be a lady barber, a cab driver, a truck driver, coal miner, smelter, derrick operator or a stevedore. (3) You will score heavily in law enforcement from Police Captain to rookie, traffic, highway patrol, warden or guard.

I predict that a new franchise will be a "School for Brides" where an ungainly young girl can be turned into a radiant bride. Social graces and bedroom manners are taught. You can expect this franchise to open near you…Canada will crack down on students who insist on "doing their own thing" which is usually anarchy…Monkeys adapt computer operations almost instantly and one of our largest insurance companies plans to use them in its billing department.

A long-lasting solid perfume will cut down your perfume expense account…Gibraltar will be big international problem again, as it has been since 711!…A new type of embalming fluid will firm up the flabbiness of the skin, restore life-like appearance even in case of long-time invalids…The sun's rays are becoming stronger, and more sun strokes will be on record next summer than any time in past half century.

I predict outraged women voters will march on Washington for equal rights in property and marriage and will also demand that the penalty be broadened for men when the crime is against women!…that a series of violent storms will strike the Atlantic Coastal areas without warning…all teachers who strike will be dismissed and their teacher's license cancelled…many open-housing societies will be forced to guarantee rent, damages, and nuisance payments.

I predict that free abortions will rapidly decrease the number of children on welfare but will increase immoral mothers…that home remedies made from herbs are fast replacing doctors in many communities…that a senator from the South will lead a campaign to restore prayer to the public schools…that teachers in New York State will be permitted to carry guns for protection.

I predict women's hats will again become a fashion rage…mounting highway accidents among younger drivers due to drugs will result in a series of road blocks within the next ninety days…the son of a famous father will inherit the fortune despite a court battle with his late father's business firm…Lady Bird Johnson will face personal criticism from fellow Democrats for her influence on LBJ as they feel it is too possessive.

I predict that June Wilkinson as the sophisticated hippie in the new TV series will be the most impersonated actress in all television next year.

Rock & Roll, Robbery, Riot, Rape, Revelry, and Drugs!

I predict a brighter tomorrow for us all! As the Scarlet Sixties end with riot, rape, revelry, murder, looting and over 1,000 assassinations internationally, we enter the Secure Seventies! Scarlet ran the river of time we called 1960-1970, but now that will change to international security, national security, state, county and city security. Yes, a brighter tomorrow!

Rock and Roll will soon have "You Have A Fat Chance Of Loving Me" and "Fat Is Beautiful" so fat will no longer be ugly and a disease, but a blessing!…That Toltec, the ingenious people-finders can discover husbands and fathers who desert wives and children in no time at all! The first question the hiding-husband asks, "How on earth did you find me?" but Toltec claims you may run away but you cannot hide!

I predict that murdercycle gangs who terrorize various areas on their motorcycles will be stopped through a new federal law…the marriage of two top cowboy stars…the daughter of a famed star who hopes to emulate her late mother's success will soon teeter on the brink of heroin addiction…that Angela Davis will become a Russian citizen next year…that three large daily newspapers will cease publication due to printing and labor costs soon.

I predict that the police will be very pleased at the rush of new laws on marijuana where no arrests are made (four joints are permitted) but a ticket given for a $100 fine! This is like a traffic ticket which must be paid at once! Any amount over four joints is a $500 fine and one year in jail and is a felony! The old arrests on marijuana was not profitable but was costly. but when the Police through the Justice Department can net $100 a ticket infraction, Justice will be served!

I predict the growing danger of the revival of the vigilantes…They were the only answer for law and order when America was younger…I predict that one of our candidates for President in the 1972 primaries will sue his doctor for malpractice as the cosmetic plastic surgery did not turn out as expected…The eternal grin will amuse too many people and lose too many votes!…Many changes from earthquakes: The Mississippi will rewind its path and the Great Lakes will shift positions.

The new drug investigations in our schools which sometimes will point to the actual sales of marijuana and heroin by the instructors themselves or sometimes the non-teaching staff! When students of only nine years old die in the school room of an overdose of heroin, speed, lsd or morphine, it is time the public became aroused…Hollywood will face a season soon with so many of her famous stars and directors passing! A tragedy at sea off the Connecticut Coast will shock us all!

I predict that the ruling of the California court declaring capital punishment is unconstitutional will set Angela Davis, Sirhan Sirhan and the Manson family free…they will be released on technicalities…The next wave of crime will come from the 15-year age group…Already these gangs are murdering, thieving and rioting…I predict that the flood gates will swing open on the entire Canadian border…All citizens crossing will be watched and searched; dogs trained to detect the mildest whiff of narcotics will be used.

I predict that the latest method of sneaking marijuana into America will be the distillation into a thick black gooey messy liquid, which can be carried in a cigar lighter or vanity case…you will soon hear about another epidemic of flying saucers and outer space mysteries…one of the better-known business managers will plead guilty and throw himself on the mercy of the court in one of the huge swindles now prevalent in Hollywood.

I predict that muggings and robberies will be on the increase due to a new set up among the dishonest where addresses and keys are exchanged! This new ring of bandits are very cleverly organized and work in precision! I predict a new breed of "fund-raisers" who will stop at nothing to collect for a charity, a church or a school! These men seek out the skeletons in family closets and then threaten to expose them to the community if a sizable sum of money is not "lovingly donated" to the cause!

I predict that the fertility pill, which results in multiple births will be the next rage among those women and girls on welfare… deaths will mount from the use of marijuana, not only in traffic accidents, but also from heart failure while the user is asleep…I predict a landmark in electric power when a $100 easy-to-install generator will be introduced from Germany and Japan for home use. The property owner can save 90 per cent of his light bill most easily.

I predict that security will be stepped up at all airports, bus stations and railways due to the increase of narcotics smuggling…a ring of men and women will be discovered who specialize in framing doctors, dentists and hospitals on malpractice charges by convincingly faking all types of physical problems and fooling even the experts…we shall soon witness a modern miracle in cures of all types—rheumatism, arthritis, etc.—by daily doses of sassafras!

Just you wait and see—I predict that money will be rationed! Too much money in circulation simply means inflation!…I predict that arson will increase with the new revolutionary idea of search and destroy…The revolutionaries who are now supported by our welfare, realize they can play the sympathy role as well as that of the destroyer! A shocking situation…There will be a federal law against all hitch hiking…Russia and China will divide up Asia.

Flow of narcotics will be checked, even linings of caskets checked, and ashes of persons cremated will be sifted when taken across state lines. Citizens of all ages are addicted to drugs…Stocks will rise high, Dow Jones reaching 1000 by late spring…Fashion notes: men will look like men, girls like girls.

In "occult folklore" marijuana was known as deadly "night-shade." It drove people out of their minds and opened them up to "demons who would take over their bodies"…In the light of modern medicine, "obsession" is a common incident when drugs, especially marijuana, is taken regularly…Senator Goldwater is pushing a new law to protect senior citizens from fraud at the hands of strangers but also from their own families!

Our water supply soon will be limited! Geologists predict that in years ahead our water will run out and this will be a parched planet…Churches, morticians, universities, civic auditoriums will face new problem, that of hiring union musicians…More crimes by hitchhikers and travel clubs warn never to pick one up; read the front pages of your newspapers.

I predict that 60 miles per hour will be the top speed an auto can achieve with the 55 miles per hour on the highway. This will conserve energy and save many human lives…in a fast and furious basketball game, three of the players will keel over dead from the overuse of narcotics. Heroin and smack can take a fearful toll…art thefts will spread to our museums and become the number one scandal. Many museums will close their doors for safety.

I predict that because of the rising crime rate in connection with hitchhiking, a new federal law will soon prohibit all hitch-hiking…all government workers, civil service or not, will have their contracts cancelled and must face the same problems as any other employee in private business…Ireland is slated to become one of the great powers of the world when the Protestants and Catholics as claimed by the Irish press "unite once and for all to drive England out of Ireland."

A full-scale war in Ireland with blood spattered over the British Isles! The Catholics and the Protestants after a bloody battle will unite and drive the British out of Ireland! Yes, Ireland will be free from the Crown after many centuries!…Chaos in India where one group will be sacrificed for another in cold blooded politics! America should refuse to send any aid to India until they return to sanity! How can we support a regime even worse than Hitler's with age old brutality rampant?

I predict you will soon learn of a shocking way which is used to smuggle cocaine and heroin into America…a dead body is procured, the rib cage, brain cavity and abdominal areas are and it is filled with narcotics, and it is accompanied by a supposed widow past customs…the body is delivered for burial, it is stripped of the drugs which are then sold on our streets…I predict that Canada and Mexico will try to tell us something when they will not permit shaggy, long haired, bearded hippies across the line.

I predict that a new federal law will demand that all drivers arrested under the influence of alcohol must spend 72 hours in jail…that weather history will be made in September…there will be a national emergency which will bring all factions together…one of our largest hospitals will be raided and closed by the Federal Narcotics Bureau for supplying illegal drugs to addicts.

Public licenses for "Rock-and-Roll" concerts will be withdrawn in many cities due to the crime and delinquency which follows the marijuana-heroin-speed narcotics at many of these events!…I predict that the Midwest will have other minor earthquakes in September-October-November!…I predict that Federal Road Blocks will be very much in operation late summer due to the increase in high-jacking and also the smuggling of drugs from Mexico!

I predict that the end of "Rock-and-Roll" will come by the end of this year and will be replaced by folk music and country-western…it will soon become known that many school children are hopeless heroin addicts at the age of nine, sometimes with teachers as pushers…the latest teenage thrill is to personally abort each other, with many deaths resulting in the coming year…it will soon be possible for you to carry a portion of ashes from the cremation of a loved one in a bracelet, ring or other jewelry.

I predict the discovery of a powerful hormone that will result in rabbits growing as large as hogs, and chickens as large as turkeys…the escape of a deadly gas from deep within the earth will tend to turn rock into a flowing lava and our bones into a jelly-like substance…long hair and beards will be forbidden in public schools, colleges and universities…also any student caught with marijuana will be expelled at once.

I regret to predict that the world is poised on a tragic event soon to happen! This ominous awesome incident will make your blood run cold…fluctuating Wall Street will simmer ever upward…Governor George Wallace will make a most important telecast, pulling no punches in denouncing the present rising crime in our cities…the coastal areas around Florida will again be the victim of 20th century pirates who converge on small pleasure ships and yachts, robbing and raping the passengers.

The dream of "recycling" (using tin cans and glass bottles over again by converting them) will fade into the dim past, as the cost is too great…Sweden will launch a drive against narcotics which is destroying the nation! In the very near future, all drug peddlers and pushers will be publicly executed on television every noon as a warning.

I predict a series of police shootings in the East will arouse America as never before!…the

deportation of over 25,000 Americans ages from 22 to 27 who are making the tourist scene

in Europe. Many of them are on forged passports…America will go on a buying spree in

October. The floodgates will open in October and a new change will come over the

nation…I predict the second series of Pentagon papers will soon find their way into print.

I predict a door-to-door search for narcotics, the users and the pushers, which will jail many

thousands and dry up the flood of marijuana, LSD, speed and heroin…the college lecture

series will gain new popularity with vibrant different personalities…a new identification

card with your fingerprints on it will be computerized for the collection of welfare

payments and in that way it does guarantee you your rightful amount. The computer is not

emotional and does not make mistakes.

I predict there is a growing drift to drugs, not only in the 13 to 18 set, but high into the

adult range of the 60's. There is a predominance of women and girls who find themselves

the hopeless victim of heroin, through the marijuana route…now that the age of 18 is adult,

the student of that age can be held for any damage he might do to any school

property…Assault and battery charges can be filed.

A conservative trend in music with Leonardo, a recently discovered voice…Hippies are

going to be rounded up and given shots for typhoid, hepatitis and an anti-drug medicine…Insurance policies can be a legalized swindle, especially if the company is a foreign one! It gives you everything in the large print but takes it away from you in the small print…Watch the speeded-up meter on the rented cars.

I predict the collapse of the United Nations within the next two years, with one nation after another walking out…Wall Street will remain the financial capital of the world…a new finding by 33 famed doctors will reveal that marijuana is not the innocent drug which some would have us believe but is the first step to heroin addiction…the American moving trend will soon shift from west to east, to the Gulf Coast states.

I predict that "mercy killing" will pass in a mid-western state and it will turn into a "merciless killing" and will prove to be a very tragic error! There is more than enough "mercy killing secretly now" let alone the circumventing of the law, openly and flagrantly! Remember that "mercy killing" will become "merciless killing" practically overnight!…I predict that the problem of the "Queen Mary" in Long Beach California going broke and the entire tourist center failing, will be saved by "public gambling" to be voted to that area!

Russia kills narcotic addicts, plans same fate for incurable alcoholics…One of greatest crimes in Russia is the unwed mother…in U.S.A. police will soon all wear plain clothes, ride in unmarked cars…Property insurance in potential riot areas will be unavailable.

Criswell's Hall of Shame for Crimes against Womanhood

(Criswell Predicts Women's Lib!)

Edwin Lee Canfield

"The world will turn to the worship of women for they will be exalted to a new high respect, love, and adoration." Nostradamus via Criswell, 1972

Criswell predicted on all manner of things, from politics to Hollywood to "shoes and ships and sealing wax, of cabbages and kings or whether the sea is piping hot or pigs have wings." One topic he frequently extrapolated beginning in the mid-1950s and through the 1970s, was womankind's eventual domination and rule over men, mankind, humankind, the World, and even Outer Space. He vividly detailed in a pulp science-fiction magazine how Mae West would be the first woman President of the United States by 1960, as well as the first person to land on the Moon with her entourage of George Liberace and Criswell himself. At one point he envisioned that pregnant women would be the first to land on the Moon. "The News reporter of the Future" was not accurate on his predictions for the Moon landing and also contrary to the beliefs of modern-day conspiracy theorists, twelve humans have visited the Moon during six missions to the

Earth's closet celestial body and the Moon landings were not an elaborate hoax

perpetrated by NASA with the help of legendary film director Stanley Kubrick.

From the June 1955, issue of the short-lived pulp magazine *Spaceway Science

Fiction*:

May we quote from the New York Enquirer, dated Sunday, May 9th, 1965? This

authentic article was by-lined by the international correspondent Charles Wireman.

Walter Winchell, Lowell Thomas, Clete Roberts, Gary Goodwin, Gabriel Heater,

Westbrook Pegler, and Sheila Graham, Hedda Hopper, Dorothy Kilgallen, Louella

Parsons, Edna Ferber and James Warner Bella all covered this take-off and return, which

was the greatest event of the 20th Century! Here is the actual report, as carefully

compiled by Charles Wireman and printed in the New York Enquirer:

"The day dawned bright and clear over the desert wasteland. There was a restless

excitement in the air. In the center of a grouping of small, low buildings, stood the

thousand-foot-long rocket, with its nose pointed ominously skyward. The name was

boldly painted on the side, 'American Lunar I.' The ground crew had been working all

night, and the signal for completion was given at 5:01:32. Exactly at 5:10:37 the official

cars arrived from Las Vegas, where they had spent three final days of planning. This

momentous event was being telecast over the entire world 24 hours a day and had been

for the past week!

There were five official cars. The first contained President West and her specially

appointed space diplomat with portfolio, Criswell. The second car contained Air Admiral

Truman, a second cousin of the former President, with his side, Counselor Arnold Lodge.

The third car carried Minister of Education, Joseph Harvard, and his aide, Frank Copley.

In the fourth car were the two Ministers of Communication for earth and lunar television,

Alvin Flanagen and Jack Heintz. The fifth car carried a representative especially

appointed by the United Nations, Orrin Delaney, and his aide, George Liberace.

The huge crowds stood in routed silence. There was no cheering,

For this was one of the most serious moments in the recorded History of Time.

Each and every individual wore a rather stern and thoughtful look, for they knew that

they were witnessing an epochal, historical event.

The ground crew stood at military attention as President West stepped from her car.

She was attired in a form-fitting, smartly-tailored space suit, which had an unnatural

gleam in the sun, like a glowing flame. She said nothing as she walked up the gangplank

and stood silently, while they attached her bubble-like helmet, and re-examined carefully

to see that there would be no atmospheric leak. The pressurized tubing was attached to

the breastplate, and President West lifted her finger to her lips, and waved farewell to the

crowd. She was followed by Criswell and the other members of the lunar expedition.

A deathly silence fell over the entire area, and only the clank of the abutting door,

and the almost inaudible hum of the propulsion as the rocket left the Earth for outer

space, were heard.

This prayerful moment was celebrated in every church, in every court, in every

school, and in every home throughout the land, by a period of silence. People kissed unashamedly on the streets: traffic stopped by itself; trains, busses, and planes interrupted their schedules; all labor stopped abruptly, for this was truly the most wonderous moment since Eternity began!"

The following is the official statement, issued by President Mae West, upon her return to Earth:

"Fear has never been in the vocabulary of a woman, and it was up to a woman to accept the challenge of space flight but a was very disappointed with the Moon! It just shows you how half the things you think are true, really aren't. I'm not going to bore you now with a long, tiresome discussion of the scientific details of this history-making first trip to the Moon, for there'll be textbooks on that from here to eternity. I hear that even the Russians are hailing me as the Columbus of Outer Space—and for the first time they admit that an American did something before they did!

Because of the extreme rarefied atmosphere of the Moon, we found no inhabitants, not even animals. The ground proved to be very spongy, but we did spot some traces of a very strange vegetation. We conducted some tests to determine the food-raising possibilities, and we are now making plans to construct air-tight buildings and attempt colonization. We are also preparing to perform the governmental ground work which will make the Moon the fifty-first state of these United States of America. We have opened new vistas for future generations. If we of the 20th Century have done nothing more than to open the Gateway to the Moon, we have done much! I want to thank each and every citizen of America, and even those who voted against me in the past Presidential election, for their fine cooperation and their interest in the future. I hereby declare, through a Presidential Proclamation, that the 9th day of May, of each year, shall be known as "Lunar Day," a national holiday. Future generations must pay respect to this great day—and those who participated in its events. When my official memoirs are published, I am sure this unforgettable adventure will be recorded for posterity!"

Criswell later walked-back on his prediction about Miss West. "No, that was misunderstood. I predicted that the first lady president would be someone like Mae West—with a magnetism for people, and who could be easily imitated." In his weekly, nationally syndicated column dated August 15, 1954, in the segment titled "What You Will Do in 1999" he began his crusade for feminism and sexual freedom with this prognostication: "By looking 45 years into the future you will find that all traces of modesty as we know it today will have disappeared, and nudity will be the accepted condition. There will be nude public bathing beaches like Europe has today and all sports arenas will feature nude racing, sports, basketball, football, track with both men and women entrants! The sexes will not be on the same level, for the women will control and own the world by that time and men will be tolerated merely for the continuation of the race. Yes, in 1999, men will bear the names of the women they marry, and woman will never give up her name for a man's. Stand by and see!"

October 31, 1954:

It is now November 1, 1999, exactly 45 years from today, and you and your family have just returned from the National Nudist Day Celebration in your local park, where everyone attended nude, in honor of this celebration. There were races, baseball games, a huge picnic, plus a huge community sing. You all had a very good time and enjoyed the perfect freedom without your clothes. On this day, everyone in this great nation, the United States (which now is composed of Canada, Mexico, Cuba, Alaska and Central America) must go nude or be fined, exactly as they are if they do not vote on Election Day. Men by this time do not vote except on minor problems, for women own and control the nation, lock, stock and barrel! Check up on this prediction!

February 6, 1955:

I predict that America will not only have a Hall of Fame, but also a Hall of Shame! This Hall of Shame will have the effects of our great criminals, who were statesmen, lawyers, doctors, teachers, soldiers, diplomats, all men, but not one woman will be represented here. All of the men in this Hall of Shame will have committed some grave crime against womanhood, rather than against humanity as a whole! Some of our national heroes who had very violent anti-feminist attitudes toward women's rights, will suddenly find themselves in the same class as the worst despots the world had produced! Yes my friend, whether you and I like it or not, 1999 will be truly a woman's world!

A rare one-sided 12-inch 78 RPM vinyl record titled *Criswell 1955* was available from local Philco television dealerships on which he recited:

"I predict that one catastrophe will follow after another in quick succession and Mother Nature will show man that she is still mistress of the Universe. I predict that 1955, will be the year of woman's supreme independence over men. She will enter and dominate the fields of politics, industry, business, medicine, and invention. I predict that in 1955, it will become apparent that there will be a woman president in 1960. In 1955, woman will control the world's largest corporation. A woman will be the most dynamic business personality of our time. A woman doctor will amaze with her new found control of glandular disturbances and a woman scientist will make the most startling scientific discovery since gunpowder."

In the February 1955, issue of *Spaceway Science Fiction*, the "20th Century Nostradamus" gazed into the future of humankind in Outer Space. He foresaw the last of the surviving human beings from Earth existing on a space station shaped like a cube:

"I predict that this floating nation in the sky will be governed not by an individual, but by an all knowing, analytical, mechanical brain. The brain will know everything there is to know, except the philosophy and psychology of the female mind…and I predict that this will cause its downfall.

Women have always been superior to men, and in this coming age will prove they are even more superior to machinery and the wizardry of so-called scientists.

I predict that tremendous floating world will be evenly divided with masculine and feminine inhabitants. All births will be controlled by artificial insemination, and the bodies of those who have died will be disintegrated. These future scientists, under the guidance of the mechanical brain, will evolve a method of isolating the life-force of all human beings—and this life-force will be kept in storage, so that each entity will have more than one chance at existence.

This cube will be divided into rooms which are all connected by a series of winding hallways, elevators, moving platforms and train service. Everything is on the inside of the cube, for the exterior will be an impregnable fortress to guard against warlike invasions from other jealous worlds, and to protect the inhabitants against the danger of meteors and cosmic rays.

I predict the life of every specimen on this manufactured planet will be as carefully controlled as the atom is today. Every thought, word or action will be policed by this tyrant brain, which will think it is greater than God. Men, women and children will be held in emotional bondage by being permitted to see only selected theatrical programs, attend carefully prepared lectures, read proscribed books, and at any time of the lunar day or night they will have their brain made a receiving station for controlled propaganda.

I predict that it will be a woman who will free all that is left of humanity from bondage under this giant monster brain.

I will now predict the actions of this brave, fearless woman, who will become known as the Joan of Arc of outer space. This amazing product of laboratory breeding will plan with her female counterparts, who are likewise convicts in the most fantastic jail ever conceived by man, a revolt against the tyrannical brain that is their warden.

I predict this is the manner in which this revolution in outer space will take place. These women will construct, in secrecy, two powerful electric generators which, at a prearranged time, will be turned on in unison. The powerful electric impulse will completely destroy the electronic brain by fusing its relays, shorting out it's circuits and shooting all its tubes, after first overcoming the brain's electronic defenses.

The men will revolt against the change of conditions, but the women will triumph for they will have the power to build a consciousness that cannot be turned by outside interference."

From his first book of predictions, *Criswell Predicts From Now to the Year 2000!* "Religion has ceased to be cultish, but there is an overall concept that everyone agrees to. The leaders of religion are women because men have misused this great truth and caused wars, privation and want! But all of man and woman's efforts to perfect this imperfect world will have been in vain, for this day, June 1, 1995, is a scant four years, two months and seventeen days before the end of this civilization we call Earth."

From a mailer-pamphlet of predictions promoting his first book:

WOMAN ON THE MOON

"I predict that this will be one of the most well-kept secrets of our generation…that

the first astronauts to the moon will be women…pregnant women! The medical fact is that

a pregnant woman can withstand more pain per square inch of her body than can a man!

Mother Nature has already pressurized her for protection, and when transported to the

Moon, would not feel the discomfort a man would! I predict that four mothers-to-be, each

schooled in taking care of each other, in various stages of pregnancy, will make the

unbeatable team of Americans who will conquer the Moon! These Mothers-to-be will not

need the extra sex stimulation and gratification that male astronauts need while in flight!"

On his 1969, 12-inch vinyl record album *The Legendary Criswell Predicts! Your

Incredible Future* he recites:

"I predict that in our tomorrow, the little women with reign supreme. I predict

that it will be impossible for a man to divorce a woman for she must divorce him. I

predict that there will not be the present marriage status, but it will be a marriage contract

by which the man must abide and if a man walks away from supporting his wife or

children, it will be a compounded felony in the eyes of justice. I predict in the future it

will be very possible for a woman to sell her husband to another woman both legally and

morally. I predict man will truly be the slave of woman. You women now control ninety-

three percent of the wealth and spend eighty-seven cents out of every dollar, so what are

we poor men to do? Personally, I welcome it because we men have made such a mess of things, you women must naturally come to our rescue and do better." He also foretold an

eventual golden age of man's subservience to woman and of another future Joan of Arc

who would rise to power after her defeat of the "Prince of Darkness" who would "turn

back the clock a thousand years. He will return women to the life of slavery and

servitude. Gone will be the vows of marriage, the right to vote, and the power of choice.

This tyrant of mankind will force woman to become the public prostitute and the servant

of the state and he alone will enjoy the monies of her shame. But this demon of greed will

not stop at the humiliation of woman…He will be overthrown and the fate of one who

dares to underestimate the power of woman, for tomorrow's Joan of Arc will lead

womankind in revolt. And then will come the golden age where there will be a woman at

the head of every nation in the world! Women will control business, finance, industry,

and will take the place of men at diplomatic tables. The conference tables and the Wall

Streets of the world. Men will take the backseat and lose their influence in your very,

very incredible future."

He presaged the sexual revolution and an era when women would be liberated

sexually as well as liberated from their clothing. "Remember, it was also a woman back

in 1448, Mother Shipton by name who foretold, 'The day of shame will come to pass, no

clothes will wear the lad or lass. Who doff the shawl, and trousers too, and romp amid the

morning dew.' Yes, Mother Shipton was quite right. Never in the history of our world,

have we dressed so briefly on the beach, in the garden, or on the streets. I predict that it

will only be a matter of time, when you will join a nudist camp or health farm and enjoy the complete freedom of nudity. The human body is nothing to be ashamed of, for we were all born in the likeness of God. And remember it will be in your lifetime, when you will walk down the street, you will shop, and you will attend the theater in the nude! And perhaps in this very same city." He follows that with a prophecy that claims that not all is lost for the male race. "I predict that you will not be able to turn this record off as they turned me off on the Johnny Carson program with my following prediction. I predict every able-bodied man in America will be asked to contribute to a sperm bank! This will later be used in artificial insemination if and when a holocaust should occur. This sperm bank will be open twenty-four hours a day and a night depository would be accepted. This for the eventuality that the male of the species might become extinct!" He concludes with "So what are we poor men to do? Personally, I welcome it, because we men have made such a mess of things that you women must naturally come to our rescue and do better!"

July 5, 1970 - THE TREND IS HERE

I predict that a ruling to be handed down by our Supreme Court in September will lift woman from servitude forever. You men may think you have just a wife now, but in September you will have a dictator. Forewarned is forearmed for this coming fray.

In his third book published in 1972, *Criswell's Forbidden Predictions Based on Nostradamus and the Tarot,* he quotes Nostradamus from when the ancient prognosticator appeared to him in a vision. "The first woman president will rule with a eunuch at her side. She will hold forth for seven years and be both hated and loved... A huge population of women from the Aegean area will unite and go against the liberation of women by being much more radical and greater tyrants. They will have nothing to do with man except to enslave him, buying and selling him like cattle. Normal sex will be outlawed and they will propagate only through artificial insemination. Huge sperm banks will be set up throughout their domain and men will be forced to make a weekly deposit."

October 2, 1971: Total Women's Lib Coming?

I predict that we men must soon face a new world of women! The Women's Liberation League will sweep every man before it, and soon! I predict that the right to vote will soon be taken from all men as they will be proven 'inferior and second-class citizens' in every state of the union! The women own and control 87 per cent of all wealth and have direct veto on the spending of 90 cents out of every dollar! I predict the women will soon hold all of the top responsible positions in law, banking, government, communication, education and transportation! We men will be at the mercy of stern hands!...Our boxers, wrestlers, football, baseball and all sports heroes will be women and the sports heroes of the past will be conveniently forgotten and written out of the records!...Any woman can win any argument over a man simply by asking, Why not give women a chance, you men have made a mess of it so far, haven't you?"

Well? . . . Haven't you??

Criswell Predicts Climate Change!

Edwin Lee Canfield

"I predict that one catastrophe will follow after another in quick succession and Mother Nature will show man that she is still mistress of the Universe."

Criswell

In a general way, a number of Criswell's predictions could be called accurate such as; shifting from paper money and coins to credit cards and other electronic forms of currency, electronic instant-delivery of mail, constantly updated news reports, increased government surveillance, tragedy and scandal for the British royal family, private companies taking over duties of the postal service, a greatly increased reliance and dependence on technology that he called "automation," the generation of "contented discontents" who only derive pleasure and satisfaction from complaining, and of course, bizarre weather, catastrophic storms, and devastating natural disasters.

As the peril to our planet increased and the awareness of its ecological destruction during the late 20th century due to human exploitation and pollution of the Earth, Criswell delivered the goods in his syndicated newspaper columns, books, audio recordings, and TV and radio appearances. "I predict that winds of a violent nature will sweep the great plains in one of the worst weather upheavals in weather history!" "I regret to predict a series of storms on the Atlantic and the Gulf of Mexico areas, some violent and some more violent! The Midwest floods! The Rockies! Late snows! The West

Coast! A small series of quakes which will bring more damage!" "When the polar ice

caps melt the world will be in for a shock! Many monsters, frozen for thousands of years

in the ice will suddenly revive and again walk the earth."

In *Criswell Predicts From Now to the Year 2000!*, he foresees "The Great Drouth

and Flood" changing the face of the earth beginning in 1977. "And I predict that the

world of tomorrow faces repeated onslaughts by the uncontrollable forces of mother

nature — more onslaughts, of a stronger type than have ever been recorded in a

comparable short span of history." "Rain will not fall for a period of ten months. I predict

that our great lakes will become beds of sand and rivers will slow down to a trickle.

Waterfalls such as the Niagara and the Victoria will be silent for there will be no water to

create their endless roars we know of today. The tides of the ocean will end, leaving huge

ships stranded and aground. This will have a far-reaching effect, for world trade will be

practically halted. When the world is struck by this horrible drouth, I predict that the

electric power will fail in many sectors for the dams which supply this energy will stand

useless and deserted and empty. Scientists will be called upon to help save human lives

for the world reservoirs will become dangerously low. Every nation will limit the use of

water. Chemicals will be used for cleansing purposes. Drinking water will be measured

for every individual and cattle will be slaughtered to prevent their death by dehydration.

You will be given so much water each day. A cupful of water which you will guard very carefully and of course, value beyond precious gems. I predict that our world faces the

worst drouth it has ever known."

He then details the death and destruction across the world caused by the great

drouth with it ending by the power of prayer. "I predict that universal prayers and

religious ceremonies will be held pleading for rain. I further predict that this drouth will

gradually cease but mother nature will shower the helpless earth with even a more

horrible disaster." "Black rain clouds of devastation will cover over Europe and the

deluge will begin. It will be slow at first with small showers each day. Later, I predict, the

rains will increase until, in time, the sun will be blacked out and rain will fall in an

endless cascade."

THE DEATH OF OUR PLANET

I predict that we have reached the point of no return in our plunder of our planet!

We have drained the oil from the under-skin of the earth, dug the metals out which gave

the earth consistence, hacked and mutilated the natural areas, tampered with the climate

by irrigation, false rivers, lakes and canals. I predict that this will take a heavy toll of

existing protective forces. The insect world, the animal world, the fish of the sea and the

plant life will prove to be no friend of ours in the final showdown, when the world will

return to a former unspoiled, unoccupied state — a point of no return!

BEGINNING OF THE END

Man will harness nature. Capture the sunlight, combine it with the atom and live

in a push button world! The Prophets of the world have predicted through trend,

precedent, pattern of habit, human behavior, and the unalterable law of cycle, that the

20th Century would be our last. No prophet predicted beyond the date of 1999! Does that

mean we will suddenly run out of time?

Even our Bible foretells the end of all the lives. So let us drink a toast to the days

that remain, so that we may live each day at a time. "Ah, make the most of what we yet

may spend, Before we too into the Dust descend; Dust into Dust, and under Dust to lie,

sans Wine, sans Song, sans Singer and sans End!

Yes, the fate of the world is in our hands. But our greed, plus the genius of

science, will destroy! The final war, the most terrible war, is at the very end of the

Ribbon of Time! But, this is not a war of man against man, nation against nation! This is a war of man against the Earth! Man, in the clutches of inhuman greed and lust, will destroy not only himself, but the very earth that gave him life! His knife plunges deeper and deeper into the heart of Mother Nature, until Mother Nature, herself, revolts against man! Just as the world was created in seven days, it will be destroyed in seven days! Mysteries of Nature held captive since the beginning of Time, will unleash hellish, pent-up silent fury.

THE DELICATE BALANCE OF NATURE: I predict that we will soon have a new cycle of bad weather! The protective skin surrounding our earth has been punctured, leaving us at the mercy of the elements of the thin cruel air of the universe! In our eager push for science, we have upset the delicate balance of Mother Nature, and she will turn on us in a wrathful manner! Remember this prediction!

"Oh my friend, coming events have already cast their shadows and whether you believe it or not, this is all to be a part of your INCREDIBLE future! Mother Nature destroys as Mother Nature creates, for this is the law of life. Time is endless and the future is only a continuation of the past!"

Flying Saucers Over Hollywood!

Charles Phillip Wireman

In early 1948, Raymond Palmer a science fiction writer and the editor of *Amazing Stories* started the pulp magazine titled *Fate*, specializing in "True Reports of the Strange and Unknown." Included in the magazine's inaugural edition was an article by Kenneth Arnold called "The Truth About Flying Saucers." Arnold recounted his 1947 encounter with a flying saucer which marked the beginning of the modern UFO era. Criswell prognosticated the future with a six-page article titled "Criswell Predicts for 1949" in the winter issue of *Fate*.

Criswell's involvement with the Flying Saucer and UFO phenomenon went beyond his predictions, columns, and role in *Plan 9 from Outer Space* (1957), He attended meetings with UFO contactees such as Orfeo Angelucci who had been contacted by beings from outer space since 1946. The meetings were first held at the Los Felix Club House and became very popular as people wanted to know more about the visitors from space. Criswell and Max Miller of the non-profit organization Flying Saucers International suggested they move to the Hollywood Hotel music room to accommodate more of the curious. The Sunday afternoon meetings became so popular that they decided to host the "World's First Flying Saucer Convention" the weekend of August 16-18, 1953. Criswell helped orchestrate the event and was the principal program moderator as well as a guest speaker. The convention was well attended and speakers included a who's who list of contactees and Ufologists including George Van Tassel, Frank Scully, Arthur

Luis Joquel II, George Adamski, Truman Betherum, John Otto from Chicago, Harding

Walsh, and a mysterious Dr. X who spoke long and eloquently on the saucers then left

immediately after speaking. The grassroots produced '*Saucers*' magazine published by

Flying Saucers International reported on the convention in the December 1953, Vol. 1 -

No. 3 issue: "You are probably well aware by now of the World's First Flying Saucer

Convention which was held by Flying Saucers International last August 16th to 18th at

the Hollywood Hotel, Hollywood, California. It has been agreed that it was a remarkable

success with impressive crowds. Best estimates at present give the approximate total

attendance at 1500. Jeron King Criswell, one of the speakers, announced that 2000 people

were turned away Monday night (the 17th) alone." The same issue of the type written

zine included the "Late News": "The following is from the October 1953 issue of 'THE

ROUNDHOUSE': "Jeron King Criswell has predicted that the government will make an

official announcement on the existence of flying saucers on December 10, 1953. He

previously said we would have space travel by 1963 because of the captured flying discs.

It has been stated that he predicted Stalin's death and the Korean truce far in advance."

Across the pond, the Autumn 1953 issue of *Flying Saucers News*: THE

OFFICIAL JOURNAL OF THE FLYING SAUCER CLUB OF GT. BRITAIN, detailed

the Hollywood convention the same way as the '*Saucers*' zine piece and Criswell's

December 10, 1953, saucer prediction as from an appearance on the TV request show

You Asked For It.

'*Saucers*' September 1954 Vol. II - No. 3, described another UFO gathering. "The next convention was called First Annual International Flying Saucer Convention— a title sounding faintly like the one we used last August—presented by a new saucer organization: Saucer Research Foundation of Los Angeles. This convention was held for three days—Friday, June 4th to Sunday, June 6th—at the Carthay Circle Theatre In Los Angeles. The theatre was large and comfortable, an excellent convention auditorium except for the transportation problem.

Of the many excellent individuals who participated were Daniel M. Fry. Orfeo Angelucci, Felix Fraser (psychic phenomena and 'The unseen Universe'), Jeron King Criswell of Criswell Predicts fame), Michael Fox (introducing reels from the science-fiction pictures 'Gog,' 'Riders to the Stars,' and 'Magnetic Monster' which were shown), and astronomer George H. Lutz (chief exponent of the metallic, not glass, mirrors for reflecting telescopes). Hal Styles was the capable moderator. There was quite a bit of audience participation."

George Van Tassel moved his family to Giant Rock, world's largest single boulder and sacred Native American ground, in the Mojave Desert near Landers, California in 1947, and opened Giant Rock Airport. In 1953 he began weekly meditation sessions in rooms underneath the rock. Soon after, he began being contacted by extra-terrestrials from Venus who landed at Giant Rock and invited George onto their ship. Onboard they gave him the technique for rejuvenating living cell tissues and plans to build a dome shaped structure called the Integratron to perform the rejuvenation techniques on which he began construction in 1954. On Sunday, April 4, 1954, the "World's First Interplanetary Spacecraft Convention" was held at Giant Rock to raise money for his project. From a platform built against Giant Rock, speakers included Orfeo Angelucci, Truman Bethurum, Daniel Fry, and George Hunt Williamson taking turns describing their contacts with physical and ethereal beings from other space. The conventions were held annually and attended by thousands until 1970 when attendance began to dwindle and bikers crashed the convention and set fire to a car. George Van Tassel died in 1978 under suspicious circumstances with the Integratron ninety-percent complete. Criswell attended the conventions lecturing and giving his predictions. He predicted that Giant Rock would be the place where World War III would begin.

William F. Hamilton III attended the conventions as well and visited Criswell at his Hollywood home. Bill worked in the information technology field for decades and studied psychology, physics, and engineering in college. He's pursued interests in science, mathematics, aeronautics, computers, and parapsychology as well as studying the UFO phenomenon since 1953. He worked as a Senior Programmer-Analyst at UCLA and was Executive Director of Astrosciences Network whose mission statement reads: "Our mission is to establish a self-sustaining, continuing research program to advance our space program, space exploration, space free enterprise, and space settlement through scientific and peaceful means, to work toward peaceful solutions to humanity's problems, and to educate the public through all recognized forms of media. To promote an ecologically viable planet earth with sustainability for all of its life forms. To establish the verified existence of extraterrestrial life, extraterrestrial intelligent life and contact and communicate with same in order to gather knowledge of, about, and from extraterrestrial entities with the goal of forming peaceful and mutually beneficial alliances." He said of Criswell, "My impression was he was a very personable man who had found a niche in televising screwball prophecies. Once he predicted on *Criswell Predicts* that giant grasshoppers were going to swarm over the Empire State Building and hit every brick, what a hoot! I guess he was just another form of entertainment."

WHB LISTENERS HEARD "JERON CRISWELL PREDICTS" ITEM ON SAUCERS September 2nd, 9:55 and 11:55 p.m. the recorded Criswell prediction broadcast said, "I predict that a new series of sightings will convince America that there is such a thing as a 'flying saucer'. Many authorities who have been silent up to date are speaking out and letting the world know in no uncertain terms that 'flying saucers' do exist. The science fiction stories of yesterday are the facts of today."

Prior to the release of *Plan 9 from Outer Space*, Criswell would claim that the film would be a new "scientific" movie that would explain the Flying Saucer and UFO phenomenon.

From his 1969, 12-inch vinyl record album *The Legendary Criswell Predicts! Your Incredible Future:* "I predict that flying saucers will officially land on the lawn of the White House to open up a new outer space inter-world treaty. Mark this date on your calendar, May the 6th, 1991."

From *Criswell Predicts From Now to the Year 2000!*:

A VISION OF SPACE

What is the secret beyond the atmospheric belt which surrounds our earth, which we call outer space?

Is the secret so terrifying that we cannot be told about it by the Pentagon?

For years we have lived with the uninterpreted visions of many great men who in their visions saw into the depths of outer space, as our newest telescopes are beginning to do, and as the sharp eye of the television camera on space vehicles are beginning to do, also.

Is it true that the keen eye of the television camera has reported floating monsters who live in the murkiness of outer space, as do sea monsters deep in the murkiness of the ocean depth?

Is it true that fallouts from atomic and hydrogen bomb tests in the stratosphere has so disturbed the creatures from outer space that they are on the verge of self-defense? What is their connection with the report of flying saucers?

Are they a part of the black rainbow that will spell doomsday for this world?

Is it possible the theory in vision is true; that these monsters of myth have at one time or another visited the earth. Is it true that far out in space, space itself becomes solid as concrete. And do these fearsome monsters inhabit the threshold of that solid world beyond our comprehension? Are scientists now burning midnight oil to fathom this mystery?

This is a vision to ponder for we stand on the verge of the unknown when we stand on the verge of space.

FLYING SAUCERS

In the vision of many men, we have seen the inhabitants of other planets who have visited our earth. I predict that these visits will increase in frequency over the next 20 years. By 1988, there will be substantiated records of visits to earth from other planets.

And, from time to time, many earth people will leave this earth to return to alien planets with the visitors from outer space. And, in the long run, these will be the lucky ones. For they and their descendants will escape the doomsday that will come on August 18, 1999.

Criswell Predicts 1999!

Charles Phillip Wireman

"Some people foretell the end of time, but the end of time will never be on time." William "Billy" Childish, 21st Century Poet

Criswell dubbed himself the "20th Century Nostradamus" and based on "trend, precedent, pattern of habit, human behavior, and the unalterable law of cycle!" claimed 87 percent accuracy in his predictions. In his 1968 book, *Criswell Predicts From Now to the Year 2000!* he predicted that the world would come to an end on August 18, 1999.

The world has yet come to an end and we are not living in the kind of future that was predicted for the 21st century in the latter decades of the 20th century. We're not living the life of the Jetsons and we have found no sign of intelligent life in the universe. Our current state of affairs could be called a cyberpunk dystopia. Or perhaps as Charles Coulombe says, "Yes, well, scoffers may scoff! But we true believers know that all of us on earth are simply dwellers in the Criswellian aftermath!"

Before Criswell predicted that his birthdate (August 18, 1907) in 1999, would be the last day for humankind, he published a huge number of predictions in his "Criswell Predicts!—An Accurate Glimpse of the Future" syndicated newspaper column during the mid-1950s, on the future wonder year of 1999. Some, well most of them, are certainly anachronous even in Criswell's twisted temporal domain. They were dated after he later predicted the date the world would end. These are excerpts from the column's segment called "What You Will Do in 1999."

August 22, 1954:

Here is what I predict you will be doing 45 years from today—in 1999: You will arise in controlled temperature, have your first breakfast snack of one pill, which will be orange juice, ham and eggs, buttered toast with jam and coffee, all contained in one tiny capsule. There will be no overweight, no sickness, no stomach disorders, for this will all be controlled through enforced diet. You will work only three hours a day at an assigned job and have the rest for relaxation. You will not permit anything to worry you, due to enforced scientific thinking, you will be free as an individual, and content with your lot! Speed the day!

August 29, 1954:

Here is what I predict you will be doing exactly 45 years from today in 1999: Diamonds will have lost their commercial value and will be used as freely for dress decorations at that time, as we use rhinestones today! The great coal mining centers will be closed down completely due to the use of solar heating and a newly introduced refined oil burning which will eliminate the use of coal altogether! There will be no smoke from factories and nothing to pollute our air. All garbage disposal will be done by chemical, and any trash will be disposed of in the same manner!…Yes, 45 years from today, another great worry will be lifted from your life: You will not be worried with headaches, for they will be overcome through a new circulatory treatment!

September 5, 1954:

In 1999, and I predict you will all live to see that day, you will have the "chance" taken out of gambling, for you will be able to have a "small electric brain" in your home which you can feed equations and get the proper answer! The right horse, the trumps in your opponent's hand, the right number on the roulette table, plus just how your mate will line up in future life! Yes, the chance will be taken out of life. A comptometer will reveal how long you will live and what disease will carry you off. The surprise will be taken out of life, and for that reason, I predict that 1999 will be rather dreary and unexciting! You and I then will look back to the good old days of 1954!

September 12, 1954:

Exactly 45 years from this very moment I predict that you will no longer have one chair in your home, you will only have reclining couches! Science will have convinced you that sitting up is bad, and if you are off your feet, you should be in the reclining position! (Never sit down when you can lie down). One other valuable lesson you will have gleaned out of the coming 45 years is that liquid soft food is much healthier than solid fried food! (Your food will come in pellets or will be liquid). Your pantry will consist of three or four jars of tiny pellets, which you can boil in water giving you thick soups, stews or meats, but if you are wise, you will be living on a liquid diet! I predict you will be alive in 1999 to check my accuracy!

September 12, 1954:

In 1999 this very newspaper will be printed on spun plastic, and when you are through reading these lines you will dip the paper in a special chemical which will soften   and clean , making you a cloth, which can be used most handily. In 1999 you will no longer be worried about the condition of your skin, your hair or personal appearance, for through the most scientific dietary compounds your system will be fed exactly what it needs for perfection. In a very public place, there will be a scale, which will diagnose your case instantly and advise you exactly what to take through a printed card. Disease will be overcome completely—overcome through an artificially induced fever which will destroy all germs and bring back normalcy overnight! Happy 1999!

October 6, 1954:

It will be a very natural event for anyone to live to be 125 years of age in 1999, because of the greatest advances Science and Medicine will make! Know that as your eyes fall on these very words there is a great possibility of you being alive in 1999! Your worries will be reduced and then you will always be young at heart, young in body, and young in mind! Your walk will be sprightly, your eyes will be bright, and there will not be an ache or pain in your body! I can safely predict that this will happen long before 1999 through Medical Science—but by that time, my friend, you can look back and see the results yourself! I fearlessly predict that we will all be together in 1999!

October 10, 1954:

The medical world of 1999 will be able to transplant any human organ and prove that the human body is made up of interchangeable parts! If you need a new lung, a new heart, a new liver or digestive tract, you will be sent to a huge clinic which is a "Bank of Human Parts" and there you will be fixed up like new! Spare arms and legs will also be available! 45 years in the future will bring us many wonders, just as the past 45 years have brought us one miracle after another! In 1999 we will all live in a safe, secure world, and until that time we will all slowly progress and humanity will improve toward perfection! Each day will bring better understanding!

October 24, 1954:

On Oct. 25, 1999, you will awake on a darkened world, for the sun will not shine in the year of 1999 due to a huge eclipse, which will be man-made! All of our atomic gases will have risen in the outer air orbit of the earth and will have solidified, making a complete ceiling, and keeping all sunlight from reaching us! Our major engineering feat of that year of 1999 will be the guided missiles we will send into outer space to explode and disperse this huge, inverted bowl of horrifying gases; I predict that we will be able to again get the sunlight, but our engineers of 1999 will be successful! 45 years will pass very quickly, so wait around and see this coming venture in space!

October 31, 1954:

It is now November 1, 1999, exactly 45 years from today, and you and your family have just returned from the National Nudist Day Celebration in your local park, where everyone attended nude, in honor of this celebration. There were races, baseball games, a huge picnic, plus a huge community sing. You all had a very good time and enjoyed the perfect freedom without your clothes. On this day, everyone in this great nation, the United States (which now is composed of Canada, Mexico, Cuba, Alaska and Central America) must go nude or be fined, exactly as they are if they do not vote on Election Day. Men by this time do not vote except on minor problems, for women, own and control the nation, lock, stock and barrel! Check up on this prediction!

November 7, 1954:

Forty-five years from this very moment, you will be looking out into a clear, happy, understanding world, for every device known to the comfort of the human race will be furnished by your government. You will have free cosmetics, free false teeth, free medical care, free vacations, free schooling, free marriage ceremonies and a free marriage bureau! The only catch is that if you want anything out of the ordinary you will be required to pay for it out of your extra money, which you will be permitted to earn, if you so desire. You will face a brave new world at that time, and life will most certainly be worth living until that time, for so many wonderful things will happen between now and then!

November 21, 1954:

On this very day, 45 years into the future, you will no longer be permitted to have any pain, due to a method of oxidizing the blood, which steps up the circulation and breaks up the congestion! Your teeth will never decay, due to a new tooth powder which will actually keep the teeth in splendid condition, plus a daily intake of three tiny tablets, which will balance the entire nervous system and direct your energies without fatigue! It will be impossible for you to gain weight, or to lose weight, for your entire system will be regulated like a clock. In 1999, you will outlast everything, rather than letting things outlast you!

December 12, 1954:

During the week of mid-December 1999, you will enjoy yourself to the utmost, for during this week, an interplanetary celebration will be held. This space festival will mark the beginning of a new era of peace and prosperity for the entire universe. We will have special telecasts from other planets. This will also mark the unveiling of a machine which will always remain in perpetual motion, alchemy or the making of gold from baser metals, the cheap manufacture of diamonds, and the complete enslavement of the atomic age! This will prove to be the greatest week in the history of the world, for man will have come of age! Please check up on this prediction personally for you will be here to do so!

February 20, 1955:

By trend, precedent, pattern of habit and the unalterable laws of science, I predict that in 1999 you will find that: (1) All disease will have been conquered by the process oxidation, (2) All climate will have been controlled by radaric principle, (3) All mental problems such as worry, fatigue, distraction and confusion will be eliminated through a brain wave machine which will banish negation of the mind, (4) All traffic on our streets, underground and in the air and in the sea, will be controlled by a rhythmic pulsation which will prohibit any accidents through collision, for each vehicle will carry its own atmospheric protection! Yes, the year 1999 could be very dull and prosaic if we allow it!

February 27, 1955:

In 44 years our world will be one of spun plastic! Yes, clear, bright, new plastic, transparent, bullet proof, shatter proof, and atomically treated for safety! You and I will move in a clean, clear world, where our very air has been washed chemically before we breathe it! Our homes, offices, theaters and churches, not overlooking the schools, will have automatically controlled dust and germ collectors which go into action when any foreign substance appears, radarically. Children will be born outside the body in a plastic pouch, and will be carried with safety, and delivered without pain or danger through the severing of the cord! Yes, we will move in a clean, clear, safe world in 1999!

March 13, 1955:

You and I will live in a controlled economy in 1999, where the price is set by an accurate forecast made scientifically, long in advance. We will know the price of wheat, corn, oats, clothing, rice, meat, rent and travel, through a cost-plus fair profit arrangement. The middleman will be out of our financial structure, and a direct method of selling between the grower and manufacturer to the consumer, will be perfected! No one will be permitted to over-indulge in alcohol or narcotics, for an instant cure will be ready to be used. We will live in a positive world which will be made possible by the lessons we will learn from 1955 to 1999! Let us speed the day!

March 20, 1955:

In only 44 years from today, you will find that there will be no "actual" delivery service for milk, butter or groceries, for it will be found that any item can be "broken down" in small particles, broadcast through the air, received at the other end, assembled and ready for consuming. Even in the year 1955, "milk" could be broadcast, but it took many years to perfect and reduce the cost of this operation! In 1999, we will also find distance has lost its charm, for we can travel any place in the world within an hour, we can reach the moon in an afternoon, and a weekend cruise in outer-space will be accepted as a thing to do, and at very reasonable rates. Yes, the more things change, the more they are the same…even in 1999!

November 3, 1957, *National Enquirer,* thru CRISWELL'S eyes YOU can see the FUTURE, Will 1999 Be the End of Everything?

"The end of the world will come," shouted the German Shepherd, "when the triangle reaches the sky!" When we examine the starry heavens and note that the three most famous planets will form a perfect triangle in 1999, we cannot help but be impressed! "The end of the world will come," wrote Nostradamus, "when the only figure in the 20th century adds to 28 and is that last figure of the 20th century!" That is 1999 - 1 plus 9 plus 9 plus 9 equals 28! "The end of the world will come," stated Pythagoras, "when three numerals are completion and one is the beginning." Nine is the numeral of completion - no single number is higher than nine. One is the numeral beginning - no number is less than one. So "when three numerals are completion and one is the beginning" could make 1999! This 1999 is only 42 years away - so it is in your lifetime and mine.

July 14, 1962—Datelines In The Future

Aug. 18, 1999: Las Vegas, Nev.

Attractions this week along the fabulous strip were Frank Sinatra, Joey Bishop, Sammy Davis, Sammy Kaye, Dean Martin, Cliff Arquette, Roberta Linn, Freddie Bell and Rudy Vallee and his roaring 20's all-star revue with Paul Whiteman, Fifi Dorsey, Helen Kane and Buster Keaton. All acts scored heavily as the new cult of personality seems here to stay! The recent musical revue from the Lunar Palace on the Moon imported by Wilbur Clark will be brought back to earth next season!

"I predict that our Geologists will soon tell you that five powerful planets may line up in opposition to Planet Earth and cancel out our delicate law of gravity! The date is the most important, so please ring this date on your calendar: August 18th, 1999! In 1544 Nostradamus warns us of this date in his 'Centuries' as the end of the world as we know it! Submerged continents could rise from the ocean floor, coastal lines could change, and tidal waves wash all the lands of the earth!"

On August 18, 1999, the world could have been very easily destroyed as NASA's Cassini spacecraft swooped past our planet at more than 42,000 miles per hour and used the Earth's gravity as a slingshot to accelerate on its way to Saturn. The Cassini contained over seventy-two pounds of plutonium fuel. If the Cassini had inadvertently entered the Earth's atmosphere, the electrical power system would have disintegrated, dispersing the plutonium so widely that 5 billion of the world population would have received ninety-nine percent or more of the radiation exposure. It would have also given everyone on earth lung cancer. NASA claimed that there was only a one-in-a-million chance that this could have occurred due to any number of malfunctions, including electrical short-circuits, meteors, or space debris striking the space probe, and erroneous ground commands. If the craft had veered even slightly from its course, it would have plunged into the Earth's atmosphere and burned up like a meteorite or like Criswell's "Vision of the End" from *Criswell Predicts From Now to the Year 2000!*

"There is a vision, which repeats and repeats and repeats. It is a black rainbow in the sky. And this black rainbow will herald the coming of the end of the world as you and I know it now. This black rainbow will encircle the planet Earth and it will be seen from every vantage point on the face of the earth for at night it will glow with an iridescent light and at day it will be a black streak across our sky; a rainbow, a jet-black rainbow; an ebony rainbow; a black rainbow, which will signify the coming suffocation of our world.

This black rainbow will seemingly bring about, through some mysterious force beyond our comprehension, a lack of oxygen. It is through this that we will be so weakened that when the final end arrives, we will go gasping for breath, and then there will only be silence on the earth. Every tick of the clock brings us nearer and nearer to this destiny."

Ending *Criswell Predicts From Now to the Year 2000!* is his final forbidden prediction for 1999:

"The world as we know it will cease to exist on August 18, 1999. A study of all the prophets—Nostradamus, St. Odile, Mother Shipton, the Bible—indicates that we will cease to exist before the year 2000! Not one of these prophets even took the trouble to predict beyond the year 2000! And if you and I meet each other on the street that fateful day, August 18, 1999, and we chat about what we will do on the morrow, we will open our mouths to speak and no words will come out, for we have no future…you and I will suddenly run out of time!"

Criswell Returns from the Grave

Edwin Lee Canfield

The Amazing Criswell was one of the first pop-celebrity psychics. His ever-present black tuxedo with sequined lapels symbolized the razzle-dazzle Hollywood showmanship that drew his loyal following throughout the mid to late 1950s. His place among the assorted cast of characters that were Ed Wood's friends, his lifelong friendship with Mae West, his unusual home life with his eccentric and provocative wife Halo Meadows, and his volumes of predictions, most extremely bizarre and inaccurate, further solidified his place amongst Hollywood's mysterious and macabre. Among his close circle of friends, he openly denied any psychic abilities and freely admitted himself to be a fraud. That sentiment was not shared among a number of his friends and associates, many of which continued to believe that Criswell did possess psychic talents. Glamour ghoul Vampira aka Maila Nurmi said, "He claimed he was not psychic. I know he was. John believed it too. But the prophecy was intended to shock. And he said, 'No, I'm not. I'm not psychic.' It was for the money was understood, it was inferred, but he didn't say it." He himself claimed he had possessed the gift of prophecy but lost it when he began to make money from it.

He prognosticated that the world would come to an end on August the 18th, 1999, also his birthdate in 1907.

On the one-hundredth anniversary of Criswell's birth, I decided to imbibe myself with a couple double Beefeater martinis, his favorite drink, at a local dive called the Zodiac Club. It had seen it's better days during the late sixties and early seventies when "What's your sign?" was a serious pick-up line. After a couple of cocktails, I began to feel lightheaded and put my head on the bar. I must have passed out for a bit and as I began to wake, I sensed someone standing next to me where there was no one before. I slowly raised my head and focused my blurred vision on the mirror behind the bar. The bar had changed. This wasn't the Zodiac Club. This place was right out of 1955. Behind me I could see where the exit from the bar entered into a plush art-deco style hotel lobby. The hazy figure standing next to me was wearing a dark suit and tie. He was sipping a martini and had a strange, large ring on the extended pinkie finger of the hand holding the glass. I raised my head more and looked toward the face. He looked familiar. Then I saw the hair. It was Criswell! Somebody must have put something in my drink. I rubbed my eyes and looked again at the reflected image in the mirror behind the bar. He was still there. I turned to my right as he turned towards me. An ominous silence filled the air, almost like the breaking point of a coming storm. His image caused me no fright, as he seemed so kind and so natural.

"Greetings my friend, I am Criswell!" he intoned.

"Yes, I know." I answered. "I'm writing a book about your life. What are you doing here?"

"I have come back from across the wounded galaxies to make my final prediction, and to thank you for the fine work you've done on my biography. I predict it will be an unprecedented success!" he replied.

"Is that your final prediction? That my book will be a success?"

He carefully explained that he was editing his predictions. "No my friend, I know that my previous prediction for the end of the world did not come to pass, but now that I am an inhabitant of the nether realms, I have more insight into coming events than when I was a mere mortal." He looked away from me, gazed slightly upward as if looking into the voidness of space and continued speaking in his stentorian, hypnotic voice. You could hear time marching ahead. I gazed into his mesmerizing, azure blue eyes and my mind became relaxed and attentive and my powers of retention became multiplied. I was suddenly removed to another time, another place. The voidness of space. Soon I was not conscious of his voice and the entire scene was a mental exchange of words. "My dear friend of the 21st century, I am in awe of your awesome future and I will tell you why. My voice trembles as I recite these lines of prophecy. Knowing in the future that a selected few of the 21st century will hear them and take heed. I somehow know that someone in the 21st century will again unfurl my banner and wave it high in honor of my forbidden prediction. Ancient Mayan mythology is intimately related to the celestial movements of stars, the Milky Way, and certain constellations. Through astronomy they developed a calendar system that was amazingly accurate. The end date of the great Mayan calendar comes at a time as a rare celestial alignment culminates. An alignment between the galactic and solar planes as the winter solstice sun conjuncts the dark-rift of the Milky Way. The Mayans believed that this rare occurrence is when the First Father, the winter solstice Sun, is birthed from the First Mother, the dark-rift of the Milky Way, creating a new world age. Mark this date on your calendar, December 21, 2012! I pass this burning torch to you to carry on in your Olympics of Life. I cannot predict what earth-shattering events will occur on this dreadful date but be assured my friend that it is all to be a part of your wondrous future."

He then looked back towards me, raised his martini in a toast and drained it dry with a smile. "Now I must go as my short time allowed on this plane of existence has run out. Good night my dearest friend, and God bless you." Before I could say anything, he turned and gracefully walked towards the exit. The sound of the song "Pomp and Circumstance" somehow swelled and filled the air. When he reached the entrance to hotel lobby he turned back, waved, and then faded away into the hotel lobby.

Next thing I knew, I was pulling my head up from the bar again and was back in the Zodiac Club. I looked up at the clock as it struck midnight. To me the incident with Criswell was no fantasy, no dream, and no imaginary voyage into non-reality. Criswell was no paper cutout, but a living, breathing human. His solidity astounded me. Was there an inter-change of souls between Criswell and myself? I will admit that I lived, read, studied, and absorbed the personality of Criswell for a number of years before I would dare to present his forbidden predictions. Did I become entranced as did Bridey Murphy, the traveler between two worlds, or an H.G. Wells, Lewis Carroll, or Jules Verne? Was I possessed by the over-powering strength of Criswell, or was it merely wishful thinking? I can deny wishful thinking as I have been most impersonal!

Criswell's prediction for the end of mankind was again wrong and he is gone…but he left behind the heritage which I now leave to you and here I have presented his final forbidden prediction as a living proof that some contact was made!

WHAT YOU WILL TALK ABOUT IN THE FUTURE!

Can your heart stand a factual report on commercialized inhuman cruelty? There are many letters on my desk from you readers appalled at the fact that the Russian scientists have succeeded in placing another head beside the normal head of a dog, and the dog is now thriving and in perfect health! This two headed dog, living and breathing in agony, is now exhibited far and wide behind the Iron Curtain! Did you know that the Russian scientists have even gone further, and have accomplished the same feat with humans? Yes, there are living, breathing agonizing humans who live today with two heads, both are practical heads, both have ears that hear, eyes that see, mouths that chew, and vocal cords that talk? The mentality is feeble, but voices, two at once, are loud and sharp! The Russian scientists have even gone further, for they have place three men, grafted them into a prison of flesh and cartilage and this monstrosity walks and talks, all sharing the same respiration and digestive tract! The same thing has been accomplished with three women who have been grafted together, and now amaze others by their crab-like walk! The other woman has been given one eye in the middle of her forehead, which works perfectly in a new man-made socket! Will these Russian scientists exhibit these man-made monsters of commercialized inhuman cruelty to our world? Russia may call this advancement, but in our eyes it is sheer terror—and your incredible future!

Criswell wrote the following terribly interesting column about food, signs of the times he lived in as a lad, and memories to make your mouth water:

"We are never strangers when we talk of food! Nine out of every ten women constantly exchange recipes. Cooking classes for men and women are the rage. We are reaching back to the magic moment of food and food alone, when all the world was very young. In the family hotel, the King house, in Princeton, Indiana, along with the Tremont Hotel in Peoria and the Mulhall Hotel in Mt. Carmel, we had the best of food for in those days you had to "set" a good table, and the competition was very heavy. Years later I would run onto past patrons of gourmet, and they would sigh with remorse about certain dishes, and the way they were prepared Indiana style. Recipes were thrown together by a pinch here, a half a cup and thorough mixing. From Germantown Chocolate Cake to Gooseberry Pies, from plum tarts to apricot spoon bread, and naturally you had three kinds of home-made bread, plus relishes, three kinds of meat, five vegetables, three kinds of potatoes, pickled beets, watermelon preserves, and two kinds of pie and ice cream. Yes, these are the memories in food of a former farm boy, later in a small town, and now a traveling journalist. I am happy to share these famous recipes with you. Try them, you can improve them by your special touch—but you won't be able to compare with the original. When I was a lad if a woman weighed less than 250 pounds she was considered puny and consumptive, and the biggest thrill outside of food was watching a fat woman climb out of a horse and buggy—those daring women in Montgomery Ward and Sears Roebuck catalogue long underwear. I still remember the food. Psychologists tell us that the taste is the key to unlocking our memory bank—and I truly predict they are right. When I recall my Indiana boyhood, my glands jump at the very thought of a favorite among all Hoosiers—Chicken Pancakes, and here is the recipe.

CHICKEN PANCAKES

1 cup sliced well-cooked chicken

2 tablespoons of scallions finely minced pinch of celery salt

1 cup of celery finely chopped

4 eggs well beaten

Pepper

Grated green pepper

Heat 4 measures of butter in frying pan. Mix beaten eggs into the rest and pour slowly into skillet. Cook over low flame until pancake is set, cut into quarters and turn each quarter carefully. Let it brown slightly, but do not overcook as the dough becomes tough. Serve at once with green peas and hot biscuits. This was the Sunday delight of the old King House Hotel for years.

THE NIGHT IS DARK

It is December 31, 1979, the night is dark and we are far from home! We are leaving the sensational seventies and into the eventual eighties! The prologue has become our epilogue, and Time has become a huge pot of seething lava! Already the clouds of more wars, more deaths, and ultimate destruction are on the horizon!

America will be invaded from within, but the mighty fortress will stand! We will emerge in 1980 without a friendly nation in the world! We will recall the words of Benjamin Franklin who told us we could not buy loyalty, respect or friendship! We will also bitterly reflect on the warning of George Washington against foreign entanglements! But it will be too late, much too late! Let us not cry out to the Heavens, but seek the peace within, our only saving grace. For we have but *twenty more years* of this world as we know it! TWENTY YEARS from 1979—in the year of 1999—all will cease.

And we will cease with it!

EPILOGUE

"And in closing I would like to say, oh my friend, when all else is lost, remember the wonderful future still remains. I'll be lonely without you and may all your shattered dreams be mended by morning and may success overtake you overnight. Goodnight my dearest friend and God bless you. Always in your future!"

Criswell

AFTERWORD

Jeron Charles Criswell King, in his own bizarre way, symbolized the nature of fame in twentieth century America. He tried unsuccessfully to break into and find fame on Broadway and Tin Pan Alley but these failures did not prevent him from co-authoring three books on how to succeed in those fields. The story of Criswell, in both his triumphs and defeats, is the story of a typically American quest for fame, and one that could not have happened without television. He had his fifteen minutes of fame long before Andy Warhol made his famous, frequently quoted observation on modern culture that rings even more true now in the twenty-first century. Since Criswell's day, the tube has created an army of celebrities who are "famous for being famous." He has the dubious honor of being one of the first. His story sheds a great deal of light on the American dream and the aspirations that most of us share. His story also asks, explores, but can't answer the eternal question of "What is the true measure of success?"

Charles Phillip Wireman, Assistant Editor

ABOUT THE EDITORS

Edwin Lee Canfield is a writer whose fascination and obsession with the life of the amazingly eccentric Criswell originated after seeing him in Ed Wood's *Plan 9 from Outer Space* and reading his first book, *Criswell Predicts From Now to the Year 2000!* This led to his authoring the 2023 book, *Fact, Fictions, and the Forbidden Predictions of the Amazing Criswell!* It was his first published book, but he has a number of projects in the works. From "laid bare" biographies to the true story of a woman murdered by human wolves, the real history of the elusive Jackalope, and a number of screenplays. He also spends time watching obscure films, exploring ghost towns, and is an avid Thanatourist. His main goal and desire as a writer is to take the title of "king of lowbrow literature" from the late, not-so-great, Leo Guild.

Canfield was born in Oklahoma, but currently resides in the desert.

Charles Phillip Wireman is a well-respected international correspondent with articles published in the *New York Enquirer* and *Spaceway Science Fiction*, as well as bylines on the AP and UPI wire services. For over three decades he served as Jeron King Criswell's Assistant Editor for his nationally syndicated newspaper columns, *Criswell Predicts* and *Dear Criswell*, earning him the title "Journalist of the Future." .

Wireman's current whereabouts are unknown.

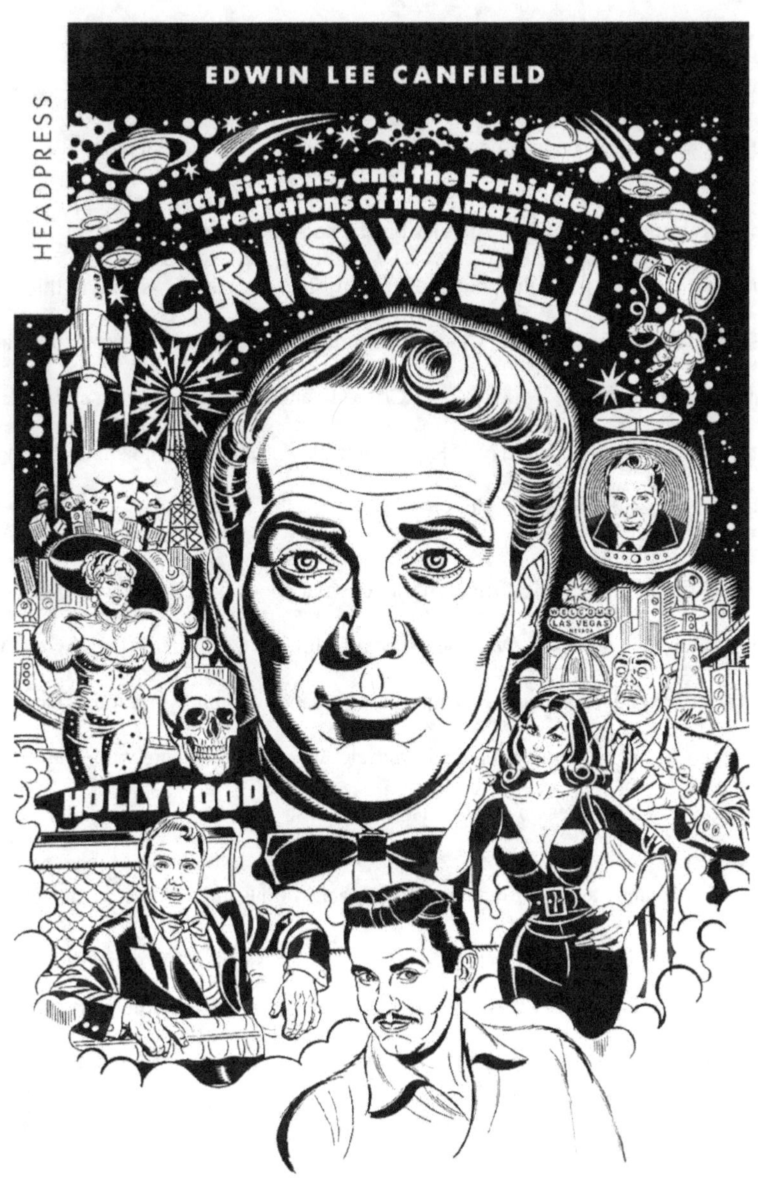
EDWIN LEE CANFIELD
Fact, Fictions, and the Forbidden Predictions of the Amazing
CRISWELL
HOLLYWOOD
WELCOME LAS VEGAS NEVADA
HEADPRESS

"Canfield cannily celebrates Criswell's bullshit while pulverizing right through it. CRISWELL PREDICTS! you will like this book on The Amazing Criswell, most assuredly a best seller of this dimension…and the next!" Rod Lott - Flick Attack

"For people who grew up in Los Angeles back when it was the old weird L.A., our imaginations were not just filled, but overfilled by The Amazing Criswell. In this obsessively researched chronicle, Canfield documents the atomic era's most fascinating charlatan. There should be a movie about Criswell, and not just Ed Wood, and this is the book the movie should be based on." K. W. Jeter - Cyberpunk and Steampunk author of Dr. Adder, Noir, and Infernal Devices

"I foresee that you will find it difficult to put down a book about a man who dared to predict on national television, while he sat next to Johnny Carson, that there would be an onslaught of 'bed bugs in Boston.' His public demeanor remained hilarious, flamboyant, and outrageous. I am so pleased that Ed Canfield has seen fit to share with us this colorful figure." The Amazing Kreskin - Mentalist and Author

"Criswell is fortunate to have found his biographer in Ed Canfield. The result of years of research, the mysterious Criswell finally emerges in all his campy glory for the reader in this affectionate biography. Canfield's writing is snappy and entertaining. He makes Criswell live again. A rewarding and enjoyable read, a must-have for all fans of Ed Wood and the surreal." Warren Beath - Author of The Death of James Dean and Who Killed James Dean?

"At last, one of 20th century America's greatest and most bizarre showmen gets his date in court. Criswell is known primarily for his association with such figures as Edward D. Wood, Jr. and Bela Lugosi; veteran writer Ed Canfield finally does justice to a man whose loyal fans included such stars of the Silver Screen as Mae West and Virginia O'Brien. He brings to a life a figure whom no one who knew can ever forget!" Charles Coulombe - Author, Lecturer, Theologian

"Edwin Canfield's extremely well researched account of Criswell's eccentric life is not only entertaining, but also reveals how Criswell's relative fame through mass-media can be seen as an innocent symptom of the beginning and continuation of the blurring of the razor-thin line between factual News and Entertainment fiction in late twentieth century America. The line which has now been all but obliterated in the twenty-first century." Charles P. Wireman - Reporter at Large – Journalist of the Future